The Royal Commission on
Historical Manuscripts

Accessions to Repositories

and Reports added to the
National Register of Archives

1988

London: Her Majesty's
Stationery Office

ISBN 0 11 440225 6

Preface

It is now nearly sixty years since the first publication of a systematic list of accessions of historical manuscripts to British libraries and record offices. Originally undertaken by the Institute of Historical Research in 1930, the list has been published by the Commission since 1954, and aims to record the more important or unusual accessions to repositories during the past year. In order to fulfil its purpose it has to be selective, and information about routine accessions should be sought from the repositories themselves or their published reports.

The continued usefulness of the publication is dependent upon its contributors, and the Commission is grateful to all those who have responded to its requests for information.

As usual, part II contains a list of numbered reports added to the National Register of Achives during the year. Some collections can be listed, and the lists forwarded to the Register, within a short time of their accession. In other cases, however, there is an inevitable delay before the production of a full catalogue, and in such cases the prompt publication of brief details in part I may be thought to be particularly valuable.

The volume has been edited and prepared for the press by Dr AR Smith, assisted by Dr NW James.

BS SMITH
Secretary

*Quality House, Quality Court,
Chancery Lane, London* WC2A 1HP

Contents

Note on access

The inclusion of material in Part I of this
publication does not necessarily imply
that it is yet available for research.
Enquiries about access should in all cases
be directed to the relevant repositories.

I: Accessions to Repositories

National and Special Repositories

ABERDEEN UNIVERSITY

UNIVERSITY LIBRARY, KING'S COLLEGE,
ABERDEEN AB9 2UB

Agnes Mure Mackenzie (1891–1955),
historian and critic: papers

Aberdeen and Orkney Episcopal diocese:
records 17th–18th cent

BIRMINGHAM UNIVERSITY

UNIVERSITY LIBRARY, PO BOX 363,
BIRMINGHAM B15 2TT

Church Missionary Society: further
records 1935–49

BRISTOL UNIVERSITY

UNIVERSITY LIBRARY, TYNDALL
AVENUE, BRISTOL BS8 1TJ

Pretor-Pinney family of Somerton
Erleigh: further accounts and papers, incl
for West Indian estates, 1566–1894

Arthur Roderick Collar, aeronautical
engineer: corresp and papers 1935–81

Victor Ambrose Eyles, geologist: MS
collection rel to history of British
geology 1679–1892, incl corresp of James
de Carle Sowerby (1787–1871) and
William Buckland (1784–1856)

Dame Katharine Furse (1875–1952),
director of WRNS: further corresp and
papers, incl some of her husband Charles
Wellington Furse (1868–1904), painter

Betty Radice (1912–85), author: corresp
and papers

Henry Willcock & Co Ltd, building
contractors, Wolverhampton: financial
records 1909–32

Bristol South East Liberal Association
minute book 1949–69

Womens Liberal Federation records
1888–1988

BRITISH ARCHITECTURAL
LIBRARY

ROYAL INSTITUTE OF BRITISH
ARCHITECTS, 66 PORTLAND PLACE,
LONDON W1N 4AD

Caroe & Martin, architects, London: job
record books 1915–78

WG Couldrey: office diaries 1882–1916

Charles Cowles-Voysey (1889–1981):
architectural drawings

WA Eden (d1975), London County
Council historic buildings architect:
research papers, mainly rel to Vitruvius
and John Carr

Erno Goldfinger (1902–87): further drawings and papers

Mewes & Davis, architects, London: drawings and designs for Royal Automobile Club 1909–22

Harold Tomlinson (d1951): architectural drawings

BRITISH LIBRARY

DEPARTMENT OF WESTERN MANUSCRIPTS, BRITISH LIBRARY, GREAT RUSSELL STREET, LONDON WC1B 3DG

Sir John Coke (1563–1644) MP, secretary of state: corresp and papers (Add MSS 64870–924)

Thomas Hopkins MP, under-secretary of state and Edward Hopkins MP, secretary to the lord lieutenant of Ireland: personal, family and official corresp and papers 1644–1793 (Add MSS 64928–29)

Thomas Clifford, 1st Baron Clifford of Chudleigh: papers rel to the secret treaty of Dover 1670 and religious and financial affairs c1660–1704 (Add MSS 65138–41)

Sir Richard Bulstrode, diplomat: further letters to him and related corresp 1675–1714 (Add MS 64950)

Nathaniel Parker Forth, stockbroker and special envoy: personal and family corresp and papers 1759–20th cent (Add MSS 65145–52)

Sir Henry Ellis, principal librarian of the British Museum: further corresp 1812–66 (Add MS 65155)

Major Charles James, author and military agent: corresp and papers 1795, 1816–18 (Add MS 64951)

Richard Cobden, politician: letters to Sir Henry Cole and others 1839–65 (Add MS 65136)

Florence Nightingale, nursing reformer (addnl): corresp with and rel to the Verney family 1870–1901 (Add MSS 68882–90)

Cadwallader John Bates, Northumberland landowner and antiquary: diary 1879–93 (Add MS 65380)

Albert Mansbridge (1876–1952), educationist: corresp and papers (Add MSS 65195–368)

Mickleton manor, Gloucestershire: map 1698 (Add MS 65102)

Battle of Ramillies sketch map 1706 (Add MS 65531)

Photographic copies of exported MSS acquired through the Department of Trade under the export licensing regulations and which became available for use during 1988 include the following:

Chronicle of England 1461–83 (RP 2040)

Sir Edward Dering (1598–1644), 1st Bt, MP: corresp and papers (RP 2162)

Sir Winston LS Churchill, prime minister: letters 1900–33 (RP 2175)

INDIA OFFICE LIBRARY AND RECORDS, 197 BLACKFRIARS ROAD, LONDON SE1 8NG

Warren Hastings, governor-general of India: further papers 1772–95, 1815, mainly rel to 1st Maratha War and his quarrel with Lord Macartney

Brown family of Anjrakandy, Malabar: family corresp and papers 1788–1927, incl corresp and papers of Murdoch Brown (1750–1828) and Francis Carnac Brown (1792–1868)

Lt-Colonel Edmund Hardy, Bombay Artillery: personal and family papers 1824–73

Jodhpur Legion (later Erinpura Irregular Force): corresp 1846–60, 1869

Robert Vernon, 1st Baron Lyveden (addnl): corresp as president of the Board of Control 1855–58

Sir Montagu SD Butler, governor of Central Provinces: family corresp and misc papers 1896–1936

George Joachim Goschen, 2nd Viscount Goschen (addnl): diaries as governor of Madras 1924–29

William George Archer (1907–79), Indian civil servant and historian: further corresp and papers

Edith How-Martyn and Eileen Palmer: diaries and papers rel to promotion of birth control in India mid 20th cent

Archibald Ian Bowman (1915–87) ICS: corresp and papers, mainly rel to war service in the Lushai Hills

BRITISH MUSEUM
(NATURAL HISTORY)

CROMWELL ROAD, LONDON SW7 5BD

Charles Dubois, treasurer of the East India Co: notes on his observation of insects 1692–95

Kenneth Page Oakley, anthropologist and geologist (addnl): letters from FA Hampton c1930–52

Mervyn Grove Palmer (1859–1955), naturalist: corresp rel to his diaries

Louis Beethoven Prout (1864–1943), entomologist and writer on music: further papers, incl journals and entomological note books and drawings

Lionel Walter Rothschild (1868–1937), 2nd Baron Rothschild: further corresp, incl some of Nathaniel Charles Rothschild (1877–1923), entomologist

Air Marshal Sir Robert HMS Saundby: entomological diaries 1943–71

Edward Saunders (1848–1910), entomologist: notes on buprestidae

Frederick Smith (1805–79), entomologist: note books, mainly rel to hymenoptera

CAMBRIDGE UNIVERSITY

DEPARTMENT OF MANUSCRIPTS,
UNIVERSITY LIBRARY, WEST ROAD,
CAMBRIDGE CB3 9DR

Thomas Walpole (1727–1803) MP: family corresp

William Darwin Fox (1805–80), clergyman: diaries

Spencer Perceval, prime minister: corresp and papers 1807–11

Elizabeth Wheler, sister of Sir Francis Galton: memoirs c1808–65

George, 2nd Duke of Cambridge: corresp 1848–92

William Holman Hunt, painter: letters to HV Tebbs 1862–74

Myles Birket Foster, painter: letters to R Dudley 1873–98

Thomas Martin Lowry, physical chemist: corresp 1915–32

Sophie, Queen of Greece: letters to RW Cole 1928–32

Reginald James White (d1971), historian: papers

Charles Osborne, author: corresp and papers c1955–85

Church Army records 19th–20th cent

UNIVERSITY ARCHIVES,
UNIVERSITY LIBRARY, WEST ROAD,
CAMBRIDGE CB3 9DR

Terrington St Clement and St John, Norfolk: estate corresp and papers 1502–1895

CHURCHILL COLLEGE,
CAMBRIDGE CB3 0DS

Michael Ashburner, geneticist: papers rel to nuclear disarmament and power c1960–65

Sir William LG Barnes (1909–87), civil servant: corresp and papers

Vernon Ellis Cosslett, (b1908), physicist: corresp and papers rel to the electron microscope

Sir Geoffrey HS Jackson (1915–87), diplomat: papers

Rear-Admiral Iain Gilleasbuig Maclean (1902–88): papers rel to naval engineering after 1945

John Ashworth Ratcliffe (1902–87), physicist: papers rel to radio wave propagation

Samuel Charles Silkin, Baron Silkin of Dulwich: legal and political papers 1974–79

Arthur Christopher John Soames (1920–87), Baron Soames: papers

KING'S COLLEGE, CAMBRIDGE CB2 1ST

John Maynard Keynes (1883–1946), Baron Keynes: further papers

Joan Violet Robinson (1903–83), economist: further papers

TRINITY COLLEGE LIBRARY, CAMBRIDGE CB2 1TQ

Edward Morgan Forster, author: further letters to Elizabeth Trevelyan 1919–56

CHURCH OF IRELAND

REPRESENTATIVE CHURCH BODY LIBRARY, BRAEMOR PARK, RATHGAR, DUBLIN 14

Stephen Gwynne, treasurer of Connor diocese: diaries 1845–73 and letter books 1861–70

Cloyne dean and chapter 1663–1904 and diocese 1680–1755 records

Church of Ireland Clergy Widows and Orphans Society: records 1863–1977

Church of Ireland Temperance Society: minute books 1879–96

DUBLIN UNIVERSITY

TRINITY COLLEGE LIBRARY, COLLEGE STREET, DUBLIN 2

Coote family, Earls of Mountrath: further estate maps for cos Leix, Offaly and Roscommon 1740

Penrose family of Riverview, co Waterford: papers 17th–20th cent

MH Gill & Son Ltd, publishers and printers, Dublin: records c1777–1879

Dr Steevens Hospital, Dublin: records 18th–19th cent

DUNDEE UNIVERSITY

UNIVERSITY LIBRARY, DUNDEE DD1 4HN

Don Bros, Buist & Co Ltd, jute and flax spinners and mfrs, Forfar: records c1805–1948

Hardie & Smith Ltd, jute spinners and mfrs, Dundee: further records 1961–85

DURHAM UNIVERSITY

UNIVERSITY LIBRARY, PALACE GREEN, DURHAM DH1 3RN

Peter Comestor, French theologian: MS of his *Historia Scholastica* early 13th cent and catalogue of the library of the collegiate church of St Cuthbert, Darlington, 1487

George Taylor (1771–1851), antiquary: commonplace books

Basil Bunting (1900–85), poet: corresp and papers of and rel to him

EDINBURGH UNIVERSITY

UNIVERSITY LIBRARY, GEORGE
SQUARE, EDINBURGH EH8 9LJ

Brian Fairfax the elder, politician: further
commonplace book and memoirs to
1685

Steuart family, baronets, of Coltness and
Goodtrees, Lanarkshire: family papers
c1623–1814, incl papers of Sir James
Steuart Denham (1712–80), 3rd Bt,
political economist

Sir David Brewster, scientist: letters (11)
1838–66

Alexander Bruce Low, son-in-law of
David Livingstone: letters and telegrams,
mainly from Nyasaland, 1874–91 and
American journal 1873

John Middleton Murry (1889–1957),
author: further corresp and papers

Arthur Koestler (1905–83), author:
further corresp and papers

Fred Urquhart (b1912), novelist and
journalist: further corresp and papers

Colin Legum, author and lecturer:
papers rel to African affairs c1950–85

Edinburgh Angling Club records
1847–1942

Edinburgh International Club records
1914–86

FAWCETT LIBRARY

CITY OF LONDON POLYTECHNIC, OLD
CASTLE STREET, LONDON E1 7NT

R May Billinghurst, suffragette: further
papers 1908–13

Charlotte Despard, suffragette and
socialist (addnl): diary of visit to Russia
1930

Shena Dorothy, Lady Simon of
Wythenshawe: corresp and papers
1920–74

Ray Strachey, suffragist: corresp with
Millicent Fawcett and papers 1916–42

Anglican Group for the Ordination of
Women: records 1932–76

National Women's Register records
c1960–88

St Joan's International Alliance, German
section: records 1952–81

Womens Forum: further records
c1950–73

Womens Provisional Club records
1924–79

GLASGOW UNIVERSITY

THE LIBRARY, HILLHEAD STREET,
GLASGOW G12 8QE

Peter Donald Thomson (1872–1955),
minister of Kelvinside (Botanic
Gardens), Glasgow: papers

Association of University Teachers
(Scotland): further records 1972–87

UNIVERSITY ARCHIVES, THE
UNIVERSITY, GLASGOW G12 8QQ

Anchor Line Ltd, Currie Line Ltd and
Donaldson Line Ltd, shipowners:
records 19th–20th cent

Babcock International plc, boilermakers
and engineers: records 1881–1988, incl
those of predecessor and subsidiary
companies

Blackie & Son Ltd, publishers, Glasgow:
further family papers 1804–59

Clydedock Engineering Ltd, ship
repairers, Glasgow: misc records
1890–1988

Thomas Hudson Ltd, boilermakers,
Coatbridge: further records 1903–86

Andrew Mitchell & Co Ltd, canvas
mfrs, Glasgow: further records 1901–77

Murray Johnstone Holdings Ltd, trust
investors, Glasgow: records 1898–1976

William Peacock Ltd, cord mfrs, Paisley:
further records 1894–1982

Smith Mirrlees, sugar machinery mfrs, Glasgow: further records c1840–1979

HOUSE OF LORDS

RECORD OFFICE, HOUSE OF LORDS, LONDON SW1A 0PW

Sir Francis Carruthers Gould (1844–1925), political cartoonist (addnl): MS autobiography.

Sir Robert Gordon Cooke MP: papers 1957–87

HULL UNIVERSITY

BRYNMOR JONES LIBRARY, THE UNIVERSITY, HULL HU6 7RX

Mervyn Aubrey Jaspan, professor of South East Asian sociology: further working papers c1950–69

Philip Arthur Larkin, poet and librarian: letters to James Ballard Sutton 1938–52

Joseph Kevin McNamara (b1934) MP, Austin Vernon Mitchell (b1934) MP, John Leslie Prescott (b1938) MP and David Julian Winnick (b1933) MP: further political papers

IMPERIAL WAR MUSEUM

LAMBETH ROAD, LONDON SE1 6HZ

General Sir Kenneth Thomas Darling (addnl): papers 1930–63

Captain JB David: papers as an Indian Medical Service officer 1942–46

Lt-Colonel L Fernley: papers as an Indian Medical Service officer in Malaya 1941–45

Captain Robert CS Garwood: naval papers 1942–46

Sir John Gibson Graham: account of his service with the Ministry of War Transport 1942–45

Captain Gilbert GP Hewett (1880–1966): naval papers, incl Somaliland operations 1920

G Holland: journal rel to her service as an ambulance driver 1914–15

Air Commodore Noel Challis Hyde: air force papers 1929–62

Captain Andrew Johnstone: naval papers 1914–19, incl service off N Russia

Captain HA King: naval papers 1919–51

Captain JWC Lancaster: papers rel to British military mission to S Russia 1919–20

Major-General Sir Arthur Lynden-Bell: letters as staff officer, Gallipoli and Egypt, 1915–16

Group Captain HR McLaren Reid: flying log books 1918–45

Major WVH Martin: papers rel to the Chindits 1944

Field Marshal Bernard Law Montgomery, 1st Viscount Montgomery: letters to Lt-Colonel T Warren 1942–70

Captain GH Roberts: naval journal and papers 1913–45

Isaac Rosenberg (1890–1918), war poet: further papers, incl letters from Gordon Bottomley 1916–18

Captain Robert ED Ryder VC, MP: naval papers 1940–45, incl some rel to St Nazaire raid 1942

Captain Lancelot M Shadwell: naval corresp and papers 1913–50

Admiral Sir Ernest CT Troubridge: diaries 1910–18

Admiral Sir William Frederic Wake-Walker: naval papers 1939–41

Lt-General Sir Richard Wapshare: diary and papers, mainly rel to the Indian expeditionary force to German E Africa 1914–15

Major HF Wheway: diary and papers rel to 22nd Dragoons in NW Europe 1944–45

Major-General Sir Thomas John
Willoughby Winterton: military papers
1929–54

Brigadier-General Charles Richard
Woodroffe: diaries as staff officer
1914–18

INSTITUTION OF ELECTRICAL ENGINEERS

SAVOY PLACE, LONDON WC2R 0BL

Michael Faraday, natural philosopher
(addnl): corresp with Benjamin Abbott
1812–19

LAMBETH PALACE LIBRARY

LONDON SE1 7JU

John Audley: precedent book attributed
to him as chancellor of York diocese
early 18th cent

Charles Marriott, tractarian: letters from
Samuel Wilberforce 1847–55

William Harrison Davey, dean of
Llandaff: corresp 1851–1901

Arthur Foley Winnington-Ingram,
bishop of London: further papers
1876–1928

John AL Riley, chairman of the Anglican
and Eastern Church Association: further
papers 1885–89

Robert Wright Stopford (1901–76),
bishop of London: papers

Inventory of Hertfordshire church plate
1915

St John Beverley Groser, master of the
Royal Foundation of St Katharine:
papers 1938–63

Sword of the Spirit movement records
1940–41

LEEDS UNIVERSITY

BROTHERTON LIBRARY,
UNIVERSITY OF LEEDS, LEEDS LS2 9JT

DH Crocker: letters from John Herbert
Le Patourel and others rel to the manor
of Bradford 1965–75

Rawlinson Charles Ford (1879–1964),
silk spinner: misc papers rel to him

Captain George Nicholls, orderly officer
to Napoleon on St Helena: corresp
1818–20

General Thomas Perronet Thompson
MP: further personal and family papers
c1745–1941

North Biddick colliery, Durham:
financial records 1722–33

Association for the Reform of Latin
Teaching: minutes 1912–73

Leeds Association of Engineers: further
minutes 1956–70

West Yorkshire Coal Owners
Association: further misc papers
1890–1948

Brotherton Collection

Thomas Blackburn (1916–77), poet:
further corresp and papers

John Gerard Braine, author (addnl):
diaries 1950–85

Bonamy Dobrée (1891–1974), English
scholar: further corresp and papers

Augustus Edwin John (1878–1961),
painter and etcher: corresp rel to gypsies

Jacob Kramer (1892–1962), painter:
further corresp and papers

Sir William Rothenstein (1872–1945),
painter: corresp

Robert Southey, poet (addnl): letters to
John May 1805–14

Anthony Simon Thwaite, poet: further
corresp 1962–66

LONDON UNIVERSITY

UNIVERSITY OF LONDON LIBRARY,
SENATE HOUSE, MALET STREET,
LONDON WC1E 7HU

Sir Douglas William Logan (1910–87),
principal of London University: papers

BRITISH LIBRARY OF POLITICAL AND
ECONOMIC SCIENCE, 10 PORTUGAL
STREET, LONDON WC2A 2HD

Edward Morris Bernstein, economist:
papers 1958–67

Duncan Lyall Burn (1902–88),
economist and historian: papers

Ely Devons (1913–67), economist:
papers

Bronislaw Kasper Malinowski
(1884–1942), anthropologist (addnl):
letters to Phyllis Mary Kaberry

Eileen Palmer, feminist: papers rel to
birth control in Palestine and the
Philippines c1930–40

Alan Richmond Prest (1919–84),
economist: papers

Lionel Charles Robbins, Baron Robbins:
papers rel to the Economic Advisory
Council 1930–32

Lt-Colonel Charles Arthur Tacey: papers
rel to the Kibbo Kift Kindred c1930–88

Richard Henry Tawney (1880–1962),
historian: further papers

Lesbian and Gay Christian Movement
records c1960–88

Union of Liberal Students: records
c1980–88

IMPERIAL COLLEGE OF SCIENCE AND
TECHNOLOGY, LONDON SW7 2AZ

Selby Angus, chemical engineer: papers
20th cent

Paul Eisenklam, chemical engineer:
papers 20th cent

Silvanus Phillips Thompson
(1851–1916), physicist: further papers

Erich Peter Wolfarth, mathematician:
papers 20th cent

KING'S COLLEGE LONDON ARCHIVES,
STRAND, LONDON WC2R 2LS

League for Democracy in Greece:
records 1945–87

LIDDELL HART CENTRE FOR MILITARY
ARCHIVES, KING'S COLLEGE LONDON
LIBRARY, STRAND, LONDON WC2R 2LS

Brigadier Philip Herbert Cadoux-
Hudson: letters from Gallipoli, the
Western Front etc 1915–26

Colonel Esmond HM Clifford
(1895–1970): papers mainly rel to E
African boundary commissions

Major-General Francis HN Davidson:
further papers, incl diary as director of
military intelligence 1940–41

Brigadier Thomas Walker Davidson:
report on his service in the Sudan
1925–31

Charles Cospatrick Douglas-Home
(1937–85), editor of *The Times*: papers

Group Captain EA Douglas-Jones:
corresp rel to the Battle of Britain 1940

Lt-Colonel WA Ebbutt: papers as
bombardment liaison officer 1944–47

Brigadier Arthur Blair Gibson (b1894):
papers rel to NW Frontier

Lt-Colonel Samuel Griffith: papers rel to
his confinement as a prisoner of war in
Germany 1941–65

Lt-Colonel Noel James: account of the
fall of Singapore 1942

Sir Charles Hepburn Johnston (1912–
86), diplomat: papers

Admiral Sir Colin Richard Keppel: scrap
books 1897–1909

William AWL Lawson, 3rd Baron
Burnham: letters from S Africa 1900–01

Brigadier-General Robert Montagu
Poore: letters from S Africa 1900–02

Lt-Colonel Roger Alvin Poore
(1870–1917): papers rel to service in S
Africa and World War I

SCHOOL OF ORIENTAL AND AFRICAN
STUDIES LIBRARY, THORNHAUGH
STREET, RUSSELL SQUARE,
LONDON WC1H 0XG

Guthrie & Co Ltd, East India merchants,
London: letter books and rubber
plantation accounts c1869–1960

John Swire & Sons Ltd, shipowners,
Liverpool: further records c1888–1964

Council for World Mission: further
records 1941–50

Presbyterian Church of England Foreign
Missions Committee: further records
1950–59

DMS WATSON LIBRARY, UNIVERSITY
COLLEGE LONDON, GOWER STREET,
LONDON WC1E 6BT

Sir William Menzies Coldstream,
painter: corresp rel to the Arts Council
1949–63

Sir Charles AL Evans, physiologist:
laboratory note books 1903–47

William Paton Ker, English scholar
(addnl): note book c1867–70

Alexander William Williamson, chemist:
corresp and papers rel to him 1927–32,
incl copies of corresp 1849–62

University College Hospital, London:
records 1812–1952

Biometrika: records of the journal
1901–16 and Biometrika Trust papers
1935

MANCHESTER UNIVERSITY

JOHN RYLANDS UNIVERSITY LIBRARY
OF MANCHESTER, DEANSGATE,
MANCHESTER M3 3EH

Hobhouse family of Hadspen House,
Somerset: corresp, incl some of Henry
Hobhouse (1854–1937) MP

Raymond CJ Howland, aerodynamic
engineer: papers 20th cent

Charles AW Manning (1894–1978),
professor of international relations:
corresp and papers

Thomas Walter Manson (1893–1958),
Biblical scholar: further papers

Norman Nicholson (1914–87), poet:
papers

Eve AE Reymond, Coptic scholar:
papers 20th cent

Sir Harold Charles Shearman (b1896),
educationist: corresp and papers

METHODIST ARCHIVES AND RESEARCH
CENTRE, DEANSGATE, MANCHESTER M3
3EH

William Harold Beales (1886–1967),
Wesleyan Methodist minister: papers

Henry Hudson (1888–1928), Wesleyan
Methodist minister and missionary:
journal and sermon register

Samuel Edward Keeble (1878–1946),
Wesleyan Methodist minister: corresp
and papers

John Rattenbury (1806–79), Wesleyan
Methodist minister: further family
corresp

Methodist Conference: records rel to
Anglican-Methodist unity and
ecumenical affairs 1955–82

NATIONAL ARMY MUSEUM

ROYAL HOSPITAL ROAD,
LONDON SW3 4HT

Thomas Mytton, Parliamentary commander-in-chief in N Wales: papers 1643–51

Lt-General Sir James AD Oughton: journals and commonplace book 1734–73

Major Charles James (1758–1821), author: corresp and papers

General Sir Eyre Coote: letters from Egypt to William Henry, Duke of Gloucester 1800–01

Major-General Hugh Lyle Carmichael: letter book as commanding officer at Guadeloupe 1810–11

Captain John Lucie Blackman, Coldstream Guards: letters to his family from the Peninsula, France and Belgium 1812–15

Mosley family of Burnaston House, Derbys: family corresp, incl letters from Captain Ashton Mosley during the 3rd Kaffir War 1851–52 and Lt Godfrey G Mosley during the Crimean War 1854–55

Lt-Colonel Charles Lygon Cocks, Coldstream Guards (addnl): Crimean War letters 1854–56

Captain Frederick Cockayne Elton VC, 55th Foot: Crimean War letters 1854–56

Frederick Arthur Stanley, 16th Earl of Derby: papers rel to the select committee on military and naval discipline 1878–79

Colonel Edward Henry Harvey, 2nd Bn, Norfolk Regt: papers 1883–1927

Christopher Birdwood Thomson, Baron Thomson: letters to his family 1902–15

Captain RS Hawker: diaries at Gallipoli and in Egypt 1915–17

Colonel Alexander Stalker Lancaster (1893–1967), military attaché at Kabul: papers

Major David WA Swannell, 3rd King's African Rifles: papers 1950–53

NATIONAL LIBRARY OF IRELAND

KILDARE STREET, DUBLIN 2

Dillon family, Barons Clonbrock: further estate papers 19th cent

Oulton family of Bagnalstown, co Carlow: papers 19th–20th cent

Thomas Clifford, 1st Baron Clifford: papers rel to settlement of Ireland c1662–72

George Bubb-Doddington, Baron Melcombe: corresp c1730

Edward Anthony MacLysaght (1887–1986), Chief Herald of Ireland: further papers

NATIONAL LIBRARY OF SCOTLAND

DEPARTMENT OF MANUSCRIPTS,
NATIONAL LIBRARY OF SCOTLAND,
GEORGE IV BRIDGE,
EDINBURGH EH1 1EW

Lindsay family, Earls of Crawford and Balcarres: further papers 14th–20th cent (transferred from John Rylands Univ L of Manchester)

Malcolm family of Burnfoot, Dumfriesshire: further papers 1701–1845

James King Annand, author: further corresp and papers 1926–85

Sir Thomas Graham Balfour, educationist: further papers 1885–95, mainly rel to Robert Louis Stevenson

General Sir Hew Whitfoord Dalrymple, 1st Bt: papers rel to his peninsular war service 1807–09

James DH Dickson (1849–1931), physicist: personal and family papers

Gavin Buchanan Ewart, poet (addnl): corresp c1974–86

Charles Grant, Vicomte de Vaux: further personal and family corresp and papers c1700–1825

Tom John Honeyman (1891–1971), director of Glasgow Art Gallery: corresp and papers

Isobel Wylie Hutchinson (d1982), botanist, traveller and author: further diaries and papers

George McArthur Lawson (1906–78) MP: corresp and papers

Malcolm MacFarlane, Gaelic scholar: corresp and papers 1891–1930

Sir John McNeill, diplomat: further corresp 1822–58

Admiral Sir Pulteney Malcolm: notes of his interviews with Napoleon 1816–17

William Matheson (b1910), Gaelic scholar: historical, genealogical and musical collections rel to the Scottish highlands and islands

Keith William Murray, Portcullis Pursuivant: working papers c1892–1909, mainly rel to the Scots Peerage

Sir Robert Murdoch Smith (1835–1900), archaeologist and diplomat: further corresp and papers

Mary FE Stewart, author: papers c1950–87

Ruth M Tait, medical missionary to China: corresp and papers 1916–49

Wilfrid Taylor, journalist: corresp and papers 1938–86

A & C Black Ltd, publishers, Edinburgh (addnl): papers rel to the publications of Sir Walter Scott c1849–1932

William Blackwood & Sons Ltd, printers and publishers, Edinburgh: further records 1952–80

Smith, Elder & Co, publishers, London: further corresp 1860–1909

Westmuir colliery, Shettleston, Lanarkshire: records 1783–97, 1849–75

Church of Scotland: further records rel to foreign missions 19th–20th cent

National Union of Mineworkers, Scottish area: further records 1911–83

Booksellers Association of Great Britain and Ireland, Scottish branch: minutes 1898–1985

Scottish National Party: further minutes 1933–38

World Day of Prayer, Scottish committee: papers 1936–89

French books of hours (3), 15th cent; English girdle book, incl notes on astronomy, astrology and medicine, 15th cent; herald's Suffolk visitation book, 1561

NATIONAL LIBRARY OF WALES

DEPARTMENT OF MANUSCRIPTS AND RECORDS, ABERYSTWYTH SY23 3BU

Somerset family, Dukes of Beaufort: further S Wales estate papers 13th–20th cent

Dannie Abse, author: further corresp and papers 1935–76

Idris Davies (1905–53), poet: further papers

Herbert Edmund Edmund-Davies (b1906), Baron Edmund-Davies: papers

Clifford Evans (1912–85), actor: papers

Tom Ellis Hooson (1933–85) MP: constituency corresp and papers

Thomas James Jenkin (1885–1965), agricultural botanist: papers

Augustus Edwin John (1878–1961), painter and etcher: further corresp and papers, incl sketch books (4) and MS drafts of his Chiaroscuro and Finishing Touches

Corporal John Griffith Jones, Wisconsin Volunteers: corresp rel to service in American civil war 1862–64

Alun Lewis (1915–44), author: papers

Sir Thomas Herbert Parry-Williams (1887–1975), poet and Welsh scholar: further corresp and papers, incl some of Amy, Lady Parry-Williams (1910–88)

William Price (1800–93), advocate of cremation: papers

John Tripp (1927–86), poet: further papers

Dafydd Wigley MP: constituency corresp 1974–83

Welsh Liberal Party records 1963–85

National Eisteddfod central office records 1977–83

NATIONAL MARITIME MUSEUM

GREENWICH, LONDON SE10 9NF

Henry Clifford, engineer: papers 1857–1905

Admiral Sir John Thomas Duckworth, 1st Bt: further papers 1795–1812

Vice-Admiral Reginald Vesey Holt (1884–1957): papers

Admiral of the Fleet Sir Geoffrey TP Hornby (1825–95), Admiral Robert SP Hornby (1866–1954) and Commander Windham MP Hornby (1896–1987): further papers

William Schaw Lindsay (1816–77), merchant and shipowner: papers

Benjamin Tucker (1762–1829), secretary of the Admiralty: papers

Admiral John Jervis Tucker: papers 1817–57

Standard Telephones and Cables Ltd, London: records c1858–1940

Royal Seamens Pension Fund records 1912–87

NOTTINGHAM UNIVERSITY

UNIVERSITY LIBRARY, MANUSCRIPTS DEPARTMENT, UNIVERSITY PARK, NOTTINGHAM NG7 2RD

Beauclerk family, Dukes of St Albans: Notts and Lincs estate vouchers and accounts c1830–39

Drury-Lowe family of Locko Park, Derbys: further legal papers 18th–20th cent

Douglas Garman, writer and communist: papers c1940–69

British Journal of Experimental Pathology minutes 1934–68

Nottingham and District Trades Council: further records c1980–88

Severn Trent Water Authority: further records, incl Nottingham City Water Department, 1852–1972

OXFORD UNIVERSITY

DEPARTMENT OF WESTERN MANUSCRIPTS, BODLEIAN LIBRARY, OXFORD OX1 3BG

Formulary, incl treatises on accounting, late 13th cent

Robert Southwell (c1561–95), Jesuit and poet: devotional exercises

Sir William Herrick, goldsmith: papers as teller of the Exchequer 1616–23

Yorkshire election canvass book 1784

Christian Charles Josias, Baron de Bunsen and Frances, Baroness de Bunsen: letters from their son Henry George Bunsen 1826–40

Sir Lancelot Shadwell, lawyer: letters 1828–42

William Beckford MP, author: letters 1843–44

Alfred Edward Hippisley, Chinese customs official: corresp and papers 1873–1940

Thomas Edward Lawrence, leader of the Arab revolt: letters to ET Leeds 1910–33

Sir Alister Clavering Hardy (1896–1985), zoologist: papers

Jack Walter Lambert (1917–86), literary editor: papers

Sir John Osbaldiston Field (1913–85),
colonial governor: diary and papers

Sir Roger JM Swynnerton, Colonial
Agricultural Service: papers rel to Malta
1942–43

Eric Lionel Mascall (b1905), theologian:
papers

Richard William Randall (1824–1906),
dean of Chichester: further papers

Nairn Transport Co, Beirut: records
c1923–50

PUBLIC RECORD OFFICE OF
NORTHERN IRELAND

Adair family of Loughanmore, co
Antrim: family and estate papers
1606–1928, incl some rel to
Carrickfergus borough

Brooke family of Dromavana, co Cavan:
corresp and misc papers 1853–1928

Cochrane and Doherty families,
Redcastle, co Donegal: further family
and estate papers 1783–1957

Crichton family, Earls Erne: further
family and estate papers 1757–1957

Dawson family, Earls of Dartrey: further
co Armagh estate and testamentary
papers 1757–1916

MacDonnell family of Belfast, Dublin
and Kilsharvan, co Meath: family
corresp and papers c1750–1920, incl
some rel to James MacDonnell
(1763–1845), physician

Reilly family of Scarva, co Down: family
and estate papers 1718–1957

John Beattie (1886–1960) MP: corresp
and papers

Charles EB Brett, solicitor, of Belfast:
papers as member of the National Trust
Northern Ireland regional committee
1935–68

Sir John and Lady Franklin: corresp,
papers and deeds 1804–1962, incl papers
rel to his search for the North-West
passage

William Graham MP: cos Louth and
Meath estate papers c1670–1770

John Hewitt, poet: papers 1904–87

Major-General Sir Oliver SW Nugent
and Catharine, Lady Nugent: corresp
c1890–1939, mainly during the Boer and
First World Wars

Nesca Adeline Robb (1905–76), author:
literary papers

McLean & Son, solicitors, Belfast: deeds
and clients papers 1767–1969

J Irwin, general merchant, Claudy:
account books 1856–1967

Central Council of Retail Licensed Trade
of Northern Ireland: minutes 1931–54

Northern Ireland 'Joint Four' Secondary
Teachers Association: minutes 1938–85

Royal Ulster Agricultural Society
records 1854–1986

Ulster Licensed Vintners Association
minutes 1872–1938

Young Mens Christian Association,
Bessbrook branch: records 1880–1950

READING UNIVERSITY

Taner Baybars, author: corresp and
papers c1960–75

Robert Henriques (1905–67), author:
corresp and papers

Hector Hugh Munro ('Saki'), author: MS poem 'Greymini' and related corresp c1913–36

Frank Arthur Swinnerton, author: letters (20) to Mrs WO Argraves 1965–72

George Allen & Co Ltd, publishers, London: records 1893–1915

Croom Helm Ltd, publishers, Beckenham: records 1972–85

Swan Sonnenschein & Co Ltd, publishers, London: letter books 1878–1911

Highfield House, Littleport, Cambs: further estate papers 20th cent

INSTITUTE OF AGRICULTURAL HISTORY, WHITEKNIGHTS, READING RG6 2AG

Goodenoughs Ltd, corn merchants, Reading: records c1910–70

National Union of Agricultural and Allied Workers: further records c1960–80

ROYAL COLLEGE OF PHYSICIANS OF LONDON

11 ST ANDREWS PLACE, LONDON NW1 4LE

Thomas Buzzard (1831–1919), neurologist: corresp, incl letters and reports on last illness of Lord Randolph Churchill

ROYAL COLLEGE OF SURGEONS OF ENGLAND

35–43 LINCOLN'S INN FIELDS, LONDON WC2A 3PN

John Thomas Quekett, histologist (addnl): diary 1842–43

Kenneth Fitzpatrick Russell, anatomist: letters to William Richard Le Fanu 1949–87

ROYAL SOCIETY LIBRARY

6 CARLTON HOUSE TERRACE, LONDON SW1Y 5AG

William Henry Dines (1855–1927), meteorologist: corresp and papers

Sir Harold Warris Thompson (1908–83), chemist: corresp and papers

ST ANDREWS UNIVERSITY

UNIVERSITY LIBRARY, ST ANDREWS, FIFE KY16 9TR

John Duncan, minister, of Scoonie: papers 1848–70

Brian ST Simpson (b1912), canon of St John's cathedral, Oban: corresp and autobiography

Charles Rodger Walker, minister, of Kemback: letters from the Near East front 1917–18

Gateside Mills Co Ltd, bobbin mfrs: records 1893–1971

Pratt's laundry, Guardbridge: wages books 1960–64

William Yule, grocer, Strathkinness: ledgers 1859–83

St Andrews Nursing and Child Welfare Association records 1922–45

Fife Medical Officer of Health: misc records 1892–1973

SCIENCE MUSEUM LIBRARY

LONDON SW7 5NH

EE Hodgkins: papers rel to ambulance seaplane service in British Guiana 1914–48

Robert Hobart Mayo (1891–1957), aeronautical engineer: papers 1913–56

Muirhead & Co, electrical engineers, Beckenham: further records 1880–1975

SCOTTISH RECORD OFFICE

HM GENERAL REGISTER HOUSE,
PRINCES STREET, EDINBURGH EH1 3YY

Fraser family, baronets, of Ledeclune, Inverness-shire: corresp, accounts and legal papers 1785–1816

Hope family, baronets, of Craighall, Midlothian: further family and estate papers 1631–1946

Sutherland family of Forse, Caithness: further family and estate papers 1620–1972

Alexander Jolly, bishop of Moray (addnl): letter books 1778–1836

Wallhouse estate, W Lothian: deeds 1559–1891

NEI Peebles Ltd, electric motor and generator mfrs: further records 1821–1980

North Leith kirk session: further records 1494–1953

Dennyloanhead Associate (Antiburgher) congregation, Stirlingshire: records 1749–96

Nicholson Street Antiburgher congregation, Edinburgh: records 1764–69

Irish National Foresters Benefit Society, Sir Charles Russell branch, Linlithgow: records 1897–1922

SOUTHAMPTON UNIVERSITY

UNIVERSITY LIBRARY, HIGHFIELD,
SOUTHAMPTON SO9 5NH

Official, naval and personal corresp and papers of Louis Mountbatten (1900–79), 1st Earl Mountbatten of Burma; naval and personal corresp and papers of Louis Alexander Mountbatten (1854–1921), 1st Marquess of Milford Haven and George Mountbatten (1892–1938), 2nd Marquess of Milford Haven; other Mountbatten family papers, incl corresp and papers of Prince Alexander of Hesse (1823–88), Julie (1825–95), Princess of Battenberg, Alexander (1857–93), 1st Prince of Bulgaria and Prince Henry Maurice of Battenberg (1858–96) and corresp of Marie Alexandrovna, Duchess of Edinburgh 1874–97; corresp and papers of Sir Ernest Joseph Cassel (1852–1921), financier and philanthropist

TATE GALLERY

TATE GALLERY ARCHIVE, MILLBANK,
LONDON SW1P 4RG

Kenneth Mackenzie Clark, Baron Clark: diaries, corresp and papers 1925–81, incl illustrations of works of art

BAR Carter, professor of fine art: corresp and papers 1962–74

Richard Ernst Eurich (b1903), painter: MS autobiography and corresp with Sidney Schiff

Maurice de Sausmarez (1915–87), painter: corresp

Adrian Durham Stokes (1902–72), author: corresp and papers

VICTORIA AND ALBERT MUSEUM

NATIONAL ART LIBRARY, VICTORIA
AND ALBERT MUSEUM,
LONDON SW7 2RL

Edward Johnston, calligrapher and letter designer: corresp with Miss Ironside 1914–18

Thomas Matthews Rooke (1842–1942), painter: memoirs

John Sparkes, artist: corresp 1869–1906

Warren Gallery, London: day book 1927–32

ARCHIVE OF ART AND DESIGN, 23
BLYTHE ROAD, LONDON W14 0QF

Georg Calmann (d1942), furniture designer: papers and designs

Natalie d'Arbeloff, artist: papers c1950–87

Sir George James Frampton (1860–1928), sculptor: papers

Edward William Godwin (1833–86), architect: further corresp and papers

Elizabeth Hake, writer on quilting: corresp and papers c1930–40

Barbara Hulanicki (b1938), fashion designer: sketch books and patterns

Eve Sandford (d1985), knitting designer: corresp, designs and samples

Marie Stevenson, needlework teacher: sewing diaries 1950–73

Edward Barnard & Sons Ltd, silversmiths, London: records 1805–1953

Calico Printers Association Ltd, Manchester: textile sample books 1933–70

International Tobacco Company of America Inc: records of advertising campaigns 1936–60

British Institute of Interior Design: records 1899–1988

UNIVERSITY OF WALES

DEPARTMENT OF MANUSCRIPTS, THE LIBRARY, UNIVERSITY COLLEGE OF NORTH WALES, BANGOR LL57 2DG

Anian, bishop of Bangor: pontifical c1266–1327

Meyrick family, baronets, of Bodorgan, Anglesey: further family, estate and literary papers c1730–1954

WARWICK UNIVERSITY

MODERN RECORDS CENTRE, UNIVERSITY OF WARWICK LIBRARY, COVENTRY CV4 7AL

Trades Union Council records c1920–60

AG Horsnail, economic analyst: papers, mainly rel to Atkinson Lorries (Holdings) Ltd shareholders committee, 1970

David Clive Jenkins (b1926), general secretary of the Association of Scientific, Technical and Managerial Staffs: papers

British Motor Industry Heritage Trust (addnl): minutes and accounts of Nuffield Group companies, incl the MG Car Co Ltd, Morris Commercial Cars Ltd, Morris Motors Ltd, Nuffield Exports Ltd, Nuffield Press Ltd, Riley Motors Ltd and Wolseley Motors Ltd, 20th cent

Coventry Precision Ltd, engineers: shop stewards committee records 1946–71

Gillot Motors Ltd, Sheffield: vehicle stock books 1932–36, 1951–57

Council of Civil Service Unions: records c1920–69

General, Municipal, Boilermakers and Allied Trades Union: misc records 1873–1973

Inland Revenue Staff Federation records 1927–52

National Graphical Association, London region (addnl): *Daily Telegraph* Imperial chapel records c1855–1987

National Union of Corporation Workers records 1907–28

National Union of Domestic Workers records 1938–53

National Union of Seamen (addnl): Isle of Man branch minutes and papers c1927–49

Union of Post Office Workers: further records 1882–1956

British Sociological Association, Medical Sociology Group: records 1970–82

Engineering Employers East Midlands Association records c1960–1988

WELLCOME INSTITUTE FOR THE HISTORY OF MEDICINE

183 EUSTON ROAD, LONDON NW1 2BP

Western MSS Collection

Thomas Gayfere, clergyman: papers rel to his insanity 1827–51

Sydney Howard Vines, botanist: letters from German botanists 1877–98

Boyd family, chemists, Taunton: prescription books and ledgers 1880–1944

Mules & Burnard, general practitioners, Ilminster: accounts 1834–49

Hunterian Society of London: further records 20th cent and MS collections

Contemporary Medical Archives Centre

Caspar Brook (1920–83), director of the Family Planning Association: papers

Hamilton Hartridge (1886–1976), physiologist: papers

George Scott Williamson (1883–1953) and Innes Hope Pearse (1888–1978), physicians: corresp and papers, incl some rel to Pioneer Health Centre, Peckham

Eugenics Society: further records 1907–78

Family Planning Association records 1921–76 (transferred from David Owen Centre for Population Studies, Univ Coll, Cardiff)

International Confederation of Midwives records c1928–88

Medical Womens Federation records 19th–20th cent

Society for the Social History of Medicine: records 1969–82

Society for Social Medicine: records 1956–82

YORK UNIVERSITY

BORTHWICK INSTITUTE OF HISTORICAL RESEARCH, ST ANTHONY'S HALL, YORK YO1 2PW

Wood family, Earls of Halifax: further estate papers 17th–20th cent

York Childrens Trust records 19th–20th cent

Local Repositories: England

AVON

BATH CITY RECORD OFFICE, GUILDHALL, BATH BA1 5AW

Walcot Wesleyan Methodist Church records 1815–1961

BRISTOL RECORD OFFICE, COUNCIL HOUSE, COLLEGE GREEN, BRISTOL BS1 5TR

William George, bookseller: antiquarian papers 1878–85

William Woodley of Clifton: deeds and papers, incl some of Strachan family, 1887–1957

Alfred Chillcott & Co, jewellers: accounts 1948–81

John Hall & Sons (Bristol & London) Ltd, glass merchants, looking glass and paint mfrs: records 1793–1988

Husbands & Sons Ltd, manufacturing opticians and photographic dealers: records late 19th–20th cent

CJ King & Sons (Holdings) Ltd, stevedores and tug owners, Avonmouth: records c1864–1950

WJ Rogers Ltd, brewers: records 1829–1963

BEDFORDSHIRE

BEDFORDSHIRE RECORD OFFICE, COUNTY HALL, BEDFORD MK42 9AP

Bassett family, bankers, of Leighton Buzzard: deeds and papers 19th cent

Thomas Shuttleworth Grimshawe, clergyman and author: financial papers 1848–50

Sir Douglas Frederick Howard (1897–1987), diplomat: personal and family papers

Usher & Anthony, architects, Bedford (addnl): records 1851–1922

Moravian Church: further records of Bedfordshire congregations 1779–1947

Wootton Charity deeds 1436–1877

BUCKINGHAMSHIRE

BUCKINGHAMSHIRE RECORD OFFICE, COUNTY HALL, AYLESBURY HP20 1UA

Rickford family, bankers, of Aylesbury: family and estate papers 19th cent

Thomas Bell, tailor, of Chalfont St Giles: papers 1798–1919

Albert Charles Chibnall (1894–1988), biochemist: papers rel to the history of the Sherington area

Francis Colmer (1873–1967), local historian: papers

John Pope Fordom, farmer, of Little Kimble: diaries 1822–33

Hudnall, Hertfordshire: deeds 12th cent–1616

Bledlow manor account book 1691–1856; court rolls of Temple Wycombe manor 1342–1544 and Winslow manor 1619–1701

Parrott & Coales, solicitors, Aylesbury: further deeds and papers 17th–20th cent

George Darlington & Sons, builders and undertakers, Amersham: further records 1889–1960

W Hearn, builder, Bourne End: accounts 1926–32

George Wigley & Sons, auctioneers and estate agents, Winslow (addnl): bidding books 1877–1934

Chearsley pre-inclosure map c1763

John Bedford's Charity, Aylesbury: further records c1756–1931

Hambleden Vale Harriers records 1908–10

Buckinghamshire poll books 1700–02 and 1784–90

CAMBRIDGESHIRE

COUNTY RECORD OFFICE, SHIRE HALL, CAMBRIDGE CB3 0AP

Pollard family of Parson Drove: family papers 1785–1839

FW Jordan: papers rel to Papworth Hospital and village settlement 1911–85

Catherine Parsons, local historian, of Horseheath: papers 1896–1946

Bacons in Thriplow manor: court roll 1678–1839

George Morling, ironmonger, Wisbech: records 1804–65

Morris family, farmers, of Oakington: farm accounts 1840–59, 1901–07

Castle Camps Congregational Church records 1813–1942

Waterbeach Drainage Commissioners records 1839–1940

Victoria County History: Cambridgeshire working papers c1950–80

COUNTY RECORD OFFICE, GRAMMAR SCHOOL WALK, HUNTINGDON PE18 6LF

Montagu family, Dukes of Manchester: further corresp and papers 1800–1971

Alconbury manor minute book 1730–40

Godmanchester manor view of frankpledge 1430

Sidney Inskip Ladds and William A Lea, architects, Huntingdon: drawings 1862–1950

St Mary and St Benedict, Huntingdon:
parish records 1574–1969

CHESHIRE

CHESHIRE RECORD OFFICE, DUKE
STREET, CHESTER CH1 1RL

Leigh family of West Hall, High Legh:
further papers 13th–20th cent

Shakerley family, baronets, of
Somerford Park: family and estate
corresp and papers 13th–19th cent

Warren-Swettenham family of
Swettenham: deeds and papers
1303–1893

James Hall, antiquary, of Nantwich:
working papers c1880–1910

Randle Holme, genealogist: pedigree roll
c1650

John S Weston, ironmonger,
Northwich: antiquarian papers
19th–20th cent

British Railways Board: accident
records, Earlestown and Crewe works,
1898–1964

Frandley Preparative Meeting, Society of
Friends: minutes 1834–1932

Cheshire Chamber of Agriculture
minutes 1868–92

Burtonwood, Lancs township and parish
council: records 1731–1970

Port of Runcorn: ship registration papers
1862–1930

CHESTER CITY RECORD OFFICE,
TOWN HALL, CHESTER CH1 2HJ

TG Burrell Ltd, department store,
Chester: records 1878–1977

Hendersons (Chester) Ltd, soft
furnishers: records 20th cent

Chester, Crewe and district Federation
of Free Church Councils: minutes
1904–07

Innholders, Cooks and Victuallers
Company records 16th–20th cent

Chester Mechanics Institution records
19th–20th cent

Chester Society of Natural Science,
Literature and Art: further records
20th cent

Chester Liberal Party records 20th cent

WARRINGTON LIBRARY, MUSEUM
STREET, WARRINGTON WA1 1JB

James Nicholson (fl 1849), local
historian: working papers

T Hulbert & Sons Ltd, flour millers,
Manchester: ledgers 1932–55, 1965–66

CLEVELAND

CLEVELAND COUNTY ARCHIVES
DEPARTMENT, EXCHANGE HOUSE,
6 MARTON ROAD,
MIDDLESBROUGH TS1 1DB

National Deposit Friendly Society,
Middlesbrough branch: minutes 1902–56

Stockton Dispensary minute book
1789–1948

CORNWALL

CORNWALL RECORD OFFICE,
COUNTY HALL, TRURO TR1 3AY

Coode family of Polapit Tamar: deeds
and plans 18th–19th cent

Treffry family of Place, Fowey: further
papers 19th–20th cent

Trelawny family of Trelawne: pedigree
1613

Samuel St John George Griffin,
clergyman: note books from 1943

Saltren Rogers, vicar of Gwennap:
corresp 1857–1908

St Eval deeds 1628–1862

Cornish Shovel Co Ltd, shovel mfrs, Hayle: records 20th cent

Harvey & Co Ltd, iron founders and engineers, Hayle (addnl): Truro branch ledgers 1935–50

Blanchminster Charity, Bude: further deeds 1744–1865

Henry Williams's Almshouse, Truro (addnl): deeds 1573–1706

Lostwithiel Turnpike Trust accounts 1774–1824

CUMBRIA

CUMBRIA RECORD OFFICE, THE CASTLE, CARLISLE CA3 8UR

Sir Henry Howard (1843–1921), diplomat: papers

Saul & Lightfoot, solicitors, Carlisle: records 17th–20th cent

Our Lady and St Joseph Roman Catholic Church, Carlisle: records 1790–1969

Duke Street United Reformed Church, Penrith: records 1824–1980

Carlisle and District State Management Scheme: further records 1916–73

CUMBRIA RECORD OFFICE, 140 DUKE STREET, BARROW-IN-FURNESS LA14 1XW

John Burnthwaite, pedlar: diary of travel through northern, midland and home counties 1830–31

James Zouch, physician, Whitehaven: note book, incl accounts of Ann Zouch, c1730–68

Broughton-in-Furness manor records 17th–20th cent (transferred from Lancs RO)

Coniston Co-operative Society Ltd: records 1908–77

Kirkby-in-Furness Co-operative Society Ltd: records 19th–20th cent

CUMBRIA RECORD OFFICE, COUNTY OFFICES, KENDAL LA9 4RQ

Thomas de Quincey, author: letters 1818–19

John Gough (1757–1825), scientific writer (addnl): MS autobiography

Sir George Mills McKay, co-founder of the English-Speaking Union: papers 1920–26

John Crosby, banker, Kirby Thore: papers 1841–49

Horrax (Ambleside) Ltd, bobbin mfrs: further records 1920–68

Westmorland & District Electricity Supply Co Ltd: records 1939

Windermere & District Electricity Supply Co Ltd: records 1934–60

Fell Pony Society records 1912–84

Independent Order of Oddfellows, Kendal district: records 1832–1937

Royal Windermere Yacht Club records 1889–1979

United Nations Association, Ambleside district: records 1963–82

DERBYSHIRE

DERBYSHIRE RECORD OFFICE, COUNTY OFFICES, MATLOCK DE4 3AG

Harpur Crewe family, baronets, of Calke Abbey: further family and estate papers 1620–1942

William Carrington, coal miner, of Ashenclough: account book 1711–57

Fairfield inclosure commissioners: note book 1772

British Rail, London Midland Region: personnel records c1920–69

Chesterfield Canal Co records 1774–1833

T & J Hutton & Co Ltd, scythe mfrs, Ridgeway: Phoenix works accounts 1891–1973

Manners colliery generating station, Ilkeston: records c1915–69

Walter Wildgoose & Sons, builders and undertakers, Bonsall: records 1887–1946

St Edmund's parish, Allestree: records 1595–1979

DEVON

DEVON RECORD OFFICE, CASTLE STREET, EXETER EX4 3PU

Fortescue family, Earls Fortescue: further Tattershall, Lincs estate papers 1782–1911

Petre family, Barons Petre (addnl): maps of Southleigh 1775 and Axminster 1778

Tayleur family of Buntingsdale, Salop: Devon estate papers 1720–1946

Sir Alexander Hamilton, sheriff of Devon: trustees accounts 1809–43

Woollcombe Watts & Co, solicitors, Newton Abbot: records 16th–20th cent, incl Highweek Feoffees

John Heathcoat & Co Ltd, lace and textile mfrs, Tiverton: records 1804–1973

Jan Reep, stockbreeder, Peter Tavy: records 20th cent

RW & FC Sharp Ltd, timber merchants and importers, Exmouth: records 20th cent

JW & W Skinner, builders and decorators, Sidmouth: records 1903–62

West of England Fire & Life Insurance Co: records 1808–47

United Reformed Church, South West province: records 1893–1966

Honiton United Charities: further records 1852–1975

Port records: Brixham registers of apprentices on trawlers 1891–1912, Dartmouth registration records 1882–1972 and Teignmouth consul's register of Norwegian and Swedish ships 1853–1909

NORTH DEVON RECORD OFFICE, TULY STREET, BARNSTAPLE EX32 7EJ

Barnstaple borough records 12th–20th cent (transferred from North Devon Athenaeum)

Clifford Rickards, chaplain of Dartmoor prison: diaries 1888–1900

Bideford & North Devon Building Society records 1853–1985

Chanters, solicitors, Barnstaple: further records 19th–20th cent

M Squire & Sons Ltd, agricultural machinery dealers, Barnstaple: records 20th cent

Braunton Independent Chapel records 1821–46

Cross Street United Reformed Church, Barnstaple: records 1772–1981

Barnstaple Bridge Trust records 16th–20th cent

Barnstaple barrack master's letter book 1784–1807

WEST DEVON AREA RECORD OFFICE, UNIT 3, CLARE PLACE, COXSIDE, PLYMOUTH PL4 0JW

Plymouth & Oreston Timber Co Ltd: records 1919–56

George Widger, picture frame mfr, Devonport: account book 1846–48

Devon and Cornwall Quarterly Meeting, Society of Friends: records 17th–20th cent

Plymouth harbour master's records 1865–89

Journal kept on board the *George and Elizabeth* 1742

DORSET

Bankes family of Kingston Lacy and
Corfe Castle (addnl): plans of Corfe
Castle c1580

Mayo family: further genealogical and
antiquarian papers 1786–1987

Pitt-Rivers family, formerly Barons
Rivers: deeds 1575–1920

Boodle Hatfield, solicitors, London:
further records 1615–1943

Farnfield & Nicholls, solicitors,
Gillingham: further records 1649–1910,
incl Gillingham manor court book
1914–25

Thomas Ensor & Son, estate agents,
Dorchester: records c1890–1969

Rural Deanery records for Beaminster
1872–1915, Bridport 1856–73 and
Dorchester 1856–1980

Bridport borough: further shipping log
books 1860–1987

Avon and Dorset River Authority:
minutes, incl predecessor bodies,
1887–1974

Shaftesbury Abbey letters patent 1442

DURHAM

Bowes manor records 1660–1982

Barnard Castle and Teesdale Methodist
Circuit: further records c1830–1939

Bowes and Romaldkirk Charity records
1805–1921

City of Durham Trust: minutes 1943–82

Durham Diocesan Family Welfare
Council: records 1917–74

Sir John Duck Charity, Chester-le-
Street: records 1910–60

Sherburn Hospital: further records
1900–71

Durham County Colliery Enginemens,
Boiler Minders and Firemens
Association: further records 20th cent

Aycliffe and Peterlee Development
Corporation records 1947–88

Durham Rural Community Council
records 1936–71

ESSEX

Belchamp St Paul manor survey by Israel
Amyce 1576; map of Berden Hall by
John Norden 1602

Great Tey: further manorial and estate
papers c1685–1954

Hilliard & Ward, solicitors, Chelmsford:
cash books and ledgers c1890–1988

GB Hilliard & Son, auctioneers,
surveyors and estate agents, Chelmsford:
further records 19th–20th cent

Braintree Baptist Church records
c1785–1978

Records of United Reformed churches at
Halstead 1718–1982, South Ockenden
1815–1977, Roydon 1798–1976,
Tollesbury 1802–1979 and Little
Waltham 1804–1965; further records of
Abbey Lane United Reformed Church,
Saffron Walden 1688–1979

Saffron Walden Horticultural Society
records 1820–1979

Boggis family, baymakers, of
Colchester: letter book 1772, 1790–91

Great and Little Clacton manor (addnl):
court books 1733–1830

Colchester & East Essex Co-operative & Industrial Society Ltd: minutes and papers 1861–1987

Lion Walk United Reformed Church, Colchester: records c1759–1987

GLOUCESTERSHIRE

GLOUCESTERSHIRE RECORD OFFICE, CLARENCE ROW, OFF ALVIN STREET, GLOUCESTER GL1 3DW

Bathurst family, Earls Bathurst: further estate maps and plans 19th–20th cent

Bazley family, baronets, of Hatherop: further family and estate papers c1850–1969, incl corresp of Sir Thomas Stafford Bazley (b1907), 3rd Bt

Blathwayt family of Dyrham Park: further estate accounts and rentals 1859–1935

Gambier-Parry family of Highnam Court: further estate corresp 1909–39

Gordon-Canning family of Hartpury (addnl): deeds 1832–1929

Graves and Graves Hamilton families of Mickleton: further deeds c1514–early 20th cent

Hanks family of Naunton: further deeds 1742–1856

Hatherell family of Oldbury-on-the Hill: farm labour book 1879–99 and farm diary 1882–85

Whitmore family of Slaughter: further diaries and papers 1789–1883

Hope Costley-White, author: papers rel to the publication of her *Mary Cole, Countess of Berkeley* c1952–87

Morgan Philips Price (1885–1973) MP: political and business papers

Horton manor rental 1665–1741 and terrier 17th–early 18th cent; Beckford manor court roll 1570 and Rangeworthy manor copies of court rolls 1708–43

Dyrham and Hinton tithe map and apportionment 1843

Rangeworthy inclosure award and plans c1811–13

Baker's mill, cloth mfr, Bisley: records c1779–1853

Bruton, Knowles & Co, auctioneers and estate agents, Gloucester: further records 1950–56

Cheltenham Cottage Co Ltd: records 1882–1937

J Coates Carter, architect, Cheltenham (addnl): papers rel to work at Prinknash Park and Westcote church 1911–17

James Creed, builder, Cheltenham: ledger 1845–54

Dancey & Meredith, architects, Gloucester: further records c1970–75

Gloucester Foundry Ltd, iron founders: records 1930–75

Edward Hayward, stonemason, Little Barrington: accounts 1897–1908

Helipebs Ltd, grinding machinery mfrs, Gloucester: records 1922–58

Henry Jordan & Co Ltd, coal merchants, Cheltenham: minutes 1914–49

Kell & Co Ltd, agricultural engineers, Gloucester (addnl): financial records 1943–55

Queen Insurance Co, Liverpool: Cheltenham agent's policy registers c1895–1943

William Seabright, builder, Cheltenham: ledger 1869–73

Tewkesbury & District Permanent Benefit Building Society: minutes 1883–1943

John Williams & Co (Cheltenham) Ltd, coal merchants: accounts and misc records 1853–1949

Wotton-under-Edge & Dursley Phoenix Permanent Benefit Building Society: minutes 1885–1966

Toc H: minutes of Gloucester 1924–75, Longlevens 1957–64, Matson 1958–71 and Shurdington 1950–53 branches and Mid-Cotswold district 1960–74

Gloucester Harbour Trustees records
1889–1974

Gloucester Pilotage Authority: minutes
1861–1984 and letter book 1924–28

HAMPSHIRE

HAMPSHIRE RECORD OFFICE,
20 SOUTHGATE STREET,
WINCHESTER SO23 9EF

Harris family, Earls of Malmesbury:
further diplomatic, political and personal
papers from 1760

Hicks Beach family, Earls St Aldwyn:
family and Hampshire estate papers
16th–19th cent

Morant family of Brockenhurst: further
estate papers 17th–20th cent

Phillimore family of Shedfield: naval and
family papers from 1780

Sturges–Bourne family of Testwood:
sketch books 1800–80

Froyle manor account roll c1200

James CM and James DK Kinnear,
general practitioners, Wickham: records
1892–1973

AG Rogers, strawberry grower,
Warsash: records 19th–20th cent

J Weeks, pharmacist, Whitchurch:
records 1917–45

Bishops Waltham United Reformed
Church records from 1836

Eastleigh Trades Council: minutes
1936–87

PORTSMOUTH CITY RECORDS OFFICE,
3 MUSEUM ROAD, PORTSMOUTH PO1 2LE

W Treadgold & Co Ltd, steel
stockholders, Portsea: records 1704–1987

National and Local Government Officers
Association, Portsmouth branch: records
20th cent

SOUTHAMPTON CITY RECORD OFFICE,
CIVIC CENTRE, SOUTHAMPTON SO9 4XR

Chessel House estate, Bitterne: deeds
1736–1842, 1911–31

RH Hammond Ltd, builders and
contractors: property management
records c1920–70

Hooper & Ashby Ltd, builders
merchants: records 1892–1968

Electrical Association for Women,
Southampton branch: records 1953–85

HEREFORD AND WORCESTER

HEREFORD AND WORCESTER RECORD
OFFICE, COUNTY HALL, SPETCHLEY
ROAD, WORCESTER WR5 2NP

Lechmere family, baronets, of Hanley
Castle: further family papers 1683–1907

HEREFORD AND WORCESTER RECORD
OFFICE, THE OLD BARRACKS, HAROLD
STREET, HEREFORD HR1 2QX

Dew family of Whitney Court: estate
papers 19th cent

Homes family, farmers, of Bosbury:
papers 19th–20th cent

Snead Cox family of Broxwood: further
deeds and papers 19th–20th cent

LW Day & Co, agricultural merchants,
Ross-on-Wye: accounts 20th cent

Golden Valley Railway Co: further
records 19th cent

Hereford city (addnl): admissions of
freemen 1659–1831

Herefordshire Fruit and Vegetable
Distribution Committee minutes
1944–49

HERTFORDSHIRE

HERTFORDSHIRE RECORD OFFICE,
COUNTY HALL, HERTFORD SG13 8DE

Braughing 1511–1749 and Pinesfield, Rickmansworth, 1807–98 manor court records: further records of Albury 1881–1926, Great Tring 1691–1708 and Park 1728–96 manors

County Fire Office Ltd, Watford: records 1828–1945

Alfred J Gentle, general engineer, St Albans (addnl): ledgers 1888–1904

Hertford and Hitchin monthly meeting, Society of Friends: further records 1688–1973

Tring Association for the Protection of Property: minutes and accounts 1824–58

Rickmansworth Conservative Association records 1923–74

HUMBERSIDE

CITY RECORD OFFICE, 79 LOWGATE,
KINGSTON UPON HULL HU1 2AA

Trustee Savings Bank, George Street branch: records 1818–1976

KENT

KENT ARCHIVES OFFICE, COUNTY HALL,
MAIDSTONE ME14 1XQ

Sidney family, Viscounts de L'Isle: further papers, incl Sir Philip Sidney's funeral roll 1588, inventories of pictures, books and plate at Penshurst and London c1622–1800 and Ingleby Greenhow, Yorks, estate map book 1764

Parish records for Hawkhurst 1579–1978 and Tunstall 1538–1979: further parish records for Kingsnorth 1538–1982 and Shadoxhurst 1538–1964

LANCASHIRE

LANCASHIRE RECORD OFFICE, BOW
LANE, PRESTON PR1 8ND

Thurland Castle plans 19th cent

Baldwin, Weeks & Baldwin, solicitors, Clitheroe: further records 19th–20th cent

Lancashire Co-operative Society records 19th–20th cent

Oglethorpe, Sturton & Gillibrand, solicitors, Lancaster: further records 14th–20th cent

Palatine Ice and Cold Storage Co Ltd, Blackburn and Palatine Food Services Ltd, Blackpool: records 1925–68

Rees & Co, chartered accountants, Oldham: further maps and plans 19th–20th cent

Storey Bros & Co Ltd, baize, leathercloth & plastic sheeting mfrs, Lancaster: further plans c1900–66

Valley Supply Co, boot factors and shoe box mfrs, Waterfoot: records c1920–49

Preston and District Power-Loom Weavers, Winders and Warpers Association: further financial records 1905–09

Royal Lytham and St Anne's Golf Club: records 1886–1986

LEICESTERSHIRE

LEICESTERSHIRE RECORD OFFICE,
57 NEW WALK, LEICESTER LE1 7JB

JH Clarke & Co Ltd, shoe mfrs, Leicester: records 20th cent

WA Spencer & Co, estate agents, Leicester: further records 19th–20th cent

Wolsey Ltd, hosiery and knitwear mfrs, Leicester: advertisement books 20th cent

Parish records of Aston Flamville 1558–1985, Blaby 1560–1986, Broughton Astley 1581–1987 and Burbage 1562–1986

Thomas Barton's Charity, Stoke
Golding: records 1615–1932

East Bond Street Working Men's Club,
Leicester: records 19th–20th cent

Workhouse Masters and Matrons
Association minutes 1900–19

LINCOLNSHIRE

LINCOLNSHIRE ARCHIVES OFFICE,
THE CASTLE, LINCOLN LN1 3AB

Booth family of Friskney: corresp
19th–20th cent, incl letters of Sir John
Franklin (1786–1847), Arctic explorer

Vyner family of Gautby: estate papers
19th–20th cent (transferred from
Cheshire RO)

Claypole survey and terrier 1730
(transferred from Newark L)

GREATER LONDON

GREATER LONDON RECORD OFFICE,
40 NORTHAMPTON ROAD,
LONDON EC1R 0HB

Charteris family: further papers, incl
Woodford, Essex and Isle of Dogs estate
papers c1841–1961

Dunsford manor court book 1874–98
(transferred from Surrey RO)

Nation Life & General Insurance Co Ltd:
minutes 1925–74

Harry Neal Ltd, building contractors, St
Marylebone: records 20th cent

Registers of the Hamburg Lutheran
Church, London 1850–1929 and the
German Evangelical Church, Islington
1858–1962

Leavesden Hospital, Hertfordshire:
records 1870–1974

London Magistrates Clerks Association
minutes 1889–1957

Thames Water Authority: records of
predecessor bodies and water companies
17th cent–1974

CORPORATION OF LONDON RECORDS
OFFICE, GUILDHALL, LONDON EC2P 2EJ

Guildhall School of Music and Drama:
further records late 19th–20th cent

City of London Mental Hospital, Stone,
Kent: records 1866–1948

GUILDHALL LIBRARY, ALDERMANBURY,
LONDON EC2P 2EJ

Thomas Bowrey, sea captain and free
merchant: further papers 1675–1712

Robert Howden Ltd, chemists:
prescription books 1863–1943

Inchcape plc: records of subsidiary
companies c1840–1968

Phoenix Oil & Transport Co Ltd:
records 1912–55

Quilter Goodison Co Ltd, stockbrokers:
accounts and letter book 1848–1948

Wallace Brothers Bank Ltd, merchant
bankers: further records c1860–1977, incl
ED Sassoon Banking Co Ltd c1930–70
and Arnhold & Co Ltd, merchants,
c1920–40

Artists Annuity and Artists Benevolent
Funds: records 1810–1979

NATSOPA and SOGAT: *Daily Mirror*
and *Sunday Mirror* day reels and machine
staff chapels records c1944–85

Life Offices Association records
1890–1976

BARNET LOCAL HISTORY LIBRARY,
RAVENSFIELD HOUSE, THE
BURROUGHS, LONDON NW4 4BE

Cooper and Arden families of Finchley:
estate papers 1865–1935

Cokayne-Frith family of Bridgen Place:
papers 1802–1900

Woodman family: papers rel to the
Hollies estate, Sidcup 1857–1930

William Everett: papers rel to Kent and
London property 1799–1940

Borax Consolidated Ltd, London:
Belvedere mills records 1899–1941

Cator family of Woodbastwick,
Norfolk: Beckenham estate papers
19th cent

HJ Furlong & Sons, estate agents,
Woolwich: records 1855–1988

Brian CJ Sedgemore MP: constituency
papers 1985–86

Berger, Jenson & Nicholson, paint mfrs,
Hackney: records 1717–1986

Gray's Mens Wear Ltd, outfitters,
Hackney: records c1925–70

CA Jacquin, button and nail mfr,
Shoreditch: business and family papers
1838–1900

Loddiges family, nurserymen, of
Hackney: records 1757–1882

Peerless Gold Leaf Co Ltd, Bow;
minutes 1934–59 and financial records
1957–70

Robert Pringle, pewterer, Spitalfields:
accounts 1886–1913 (transferred from
Geffrye Mus)

Mare Street Baptist Church, Hackney:
records 1798–1988

Hackney Benevolent Pension Society:
further records 1921–61

Anne, Lady Rose, of Walworth: further
papers c1780–1820

Southwark Cathedral records
c1890–1975

South London Mission Circuit records
1850–1981

Princelet Street Synagogue records
1883–1973

Stepney Meeting House
(Congregationalist): records 1644–1974

Colsell family of Leytonstone: corresp
rel to archaeological fieldwork in
Guatemala c1906

Jenny Hammond (1894–1988), mayor of
Leyton: political and autobiographical
papers

Walter Frederick Gulliver, pharmacist:
records 1831–1912

George Smith & Sons Ltd, manufacturing furriers: records 1873–1987

Wager Tayler, hatter: memorandum and account book 1791–95

GREATER MANCHESTER

GREATER MANCHESTER COUNTY RECORD OFFICE, 56 MARSHALL STREET, NEW CROSS, MANCHESTER M4 5FU

Legh family of Lyme Park, Cheshire: family and estate papers 18th–19th cent

Harold Greenwood, architect: papers 1867–1929

D & H Mallalieu Ltd, woollen mfrs, Delph, Yorkshire: records 19th–20th cent

Oldham Photographic Society records 1867–1967

Greater Manchester Labour Party records c1974–88

MANCHESTER CENTRAL LIBRARY ARCHIVES DEPARTMENT, ST PETER'S SQUARE, MANCHESTER M2 5PD

J Garland Long: papers rel to Legion of Frontiersmen 1905–18

Barnes Samaritan Charity minutes 1872–1982

Cotton Districts Convalescent Fund: minutes 1875–1976

Manchester & Salford Ragged School Union: records 1858–1972

Manchester Sacred Song Association: minutes 1881–1975

BOLTON ARCHIVE SERVICE, CENTRAL LIBRARY, CIVIC CENTRE, LE MANS CRESCENT, BOLTON BL1 1SE

Richard Harwood & Son Ltd, cotton spinners: records c1920–70

Manchester, Bolton & Bury Canal Co: further records 1893–1963

Spence & Co (Bookbinders) Ltd, manufacturing stationers: records c1930–70

Tillotson & Son Ltd, printers, publishers and proprietors of the *Bolton Evening News*: records c1865–1960, incl corresp of William Frederic Tillotson (1844–89)

Westhoughton United Industrial Co-operative Society Ltd: accounts and papers 1871–1915

Bolton Committee for the Reclamation of Unfortunate Women: records c1865–70

Co-operative Womens Guild, Bolton: records 1889–1970

BURY ARCHIVE SERVICE, 22A UNION ARCADE, BURY BL9 0QF

Amalgamated Union of Engineering Workers, Bury and Heywood district: records 1920–86

Bury North Liberal Association records 1960–80

SALFORD ARCHIVES CENTRE, 658/662 LIVERPOOL ROAD, IRLAM, MANCHESTER M30 5AD

Leigh family of Worsley: deeds 1701–1816

Clifton and Kersley Mutual Improvement Society: minutes 1861–1926

STOCKPORT ARCHIVE SERVICE, CENTRAL LIBRARY, WELLINGTON ROAD SOUTH, STOCKPORT SK1 3RS

Sir Ralph Pendlebury's Charity for Orphans: records 1870–1980

J Blundell & Son, coal proprietors:
registers of damages 1892–1929

Harrison, McGregor & Guest Ltd,
agricultural equipment mfrs, Leigh
(addnl): records 1875–20th cent

Manchester Collieries Ltd: leasehold
royalty accounts 1936–46

Tyldesley Coal Co Ltd: records 1870–95

Orrell and Lamberhead Green Methodist
Circuit: further records 1852–1987

Ashton in Makerfield Grammar School
and charities: records 1590–1951

Wigan Grammar School: further records
1891–1972

Wigan Trades Council and Wigan
Labour Party: records 1921–70

MERSEYSIDE

Joseph Heap & Sons Ltd, rice millers:
records 1900–74

John Holt & Co (Liverpool) Ltd, West
Africa merchants: records 1882–1980,
incl subsidiary companies

L Keizer & Co Ltd, glass merchants:
records 1903–50

Lamport & Holt Line Ltd, shipowners:
records 19th–20th cent

Edward W Turner & Son (Liverpool)
Ltd, ship brokers: records c1866–1982

Liverpool Provision Trade Association
records c1874–1950

Training ship Conway: records 20th cent

Sir John Gladstone, 1st Bt, merchant and
MP: bills and receipts rel to South
American trade 1811–12

Cyril Taylor, general practitioner: papers
rel to the Merrison Commission on the
National Health Service 1976–79

Dame Ethel May Wormald, lord mayor
of Liverpool: papers c1950–88

RJ Tilney & Co, stockbrokers: further
ledgers 19th–20th cent

Florence Institute for Boys: records
1880–1988

Walton workhouse chaplain's books
1901–18

Birkenhead Medical Society records
1856–1981

Soroptimist International, Birkenhead
club: records 1933–84

Wirral Footpaths and Open Spaces
Preservation Society: records 1888–1987

WEST MIDLANDS

Albright family: corresp and papers
18th–20th cent

Parker-Jervis family, Viscounts St
Vincent: corresp and papers 18th cent,
mainly rel to the Jacobite rising of 1745

Imperial Metal Industries Ltd: records
19th cent–1962, incl subsidiary
companies

Birmingham Exchange: minutes
1861–1978

West Midlands Advisory Council for Further Education: minutes 1895–1976

COVENTRY CITY RECORD OFFICE, BAYLEY LANE, COVENTRY CV1 5RG

Charles Ager Ltd, shoe makers and retailers: records 20th cent

Clarke, Cluley & Co, aeronautical engineers and agricultural machinery mfrs, Kenilworth: records 1899–1979

Coventry Movement Co Ltd, watch mfrs: further records 1889–1986

ET Peirson & Sons, accountants: records 1904–70

Wickman Ltd, machine tool mfrs: further records 1940–80

Queen's Road Baptist Church records 18th–20th cent

Samuel Smith's Charity records 1761–1964

Amalgamated Union of Engineering Workers, Coventry district: records 1898–1983

Birmingham and District Clerks Provident Association, Coventry office: subscription books 1932–58

Coventry Working Mens Club (addnl): deeds 17th–20th cent and minutes 1947–69

National Council of Women, Coventry branch: records 1934–88

Social Democratic Party, Coventry area: records from c1981

DUDLEY ARCHIVES AND LOCAL HISTORY DEPARTMENT, DUDLEY LIBRARY, ST JAMES'S ROAD, DUDLEY DY1 1HR

John Bradley & Co (Stourbridge) Ltd, iron founders: further records 20th cent

Brettell Lane Foundry Ltd, iron founders, Brierley Hill: records 20th cent

Chain Developments Ltd, chain mfrs, Netherton: further records 20th cent

Halesowen Brick & Tile Co: further records 20th cent

Hart's Hill Iron Co Ltd, iron mfrs, Brierley Hill: further records 19th–20th cent

N Hingley & Sons Ltd, iron mfrs, Netherton: further records 20th cent

Stourbridge Model Laundry Ltd: minutes 1897–1937

Associated Society of Locomotive Engineers and Firemen, Stourbridge branch: further records 20th cent

Wrought Hollow-Ware Trade Employers Association minutes 1915–73

WALSALL ARCHIVES SERVICE, LOCAL HISTORY CENTRE, ESSEX STREET, WALSALL WS2 7AS

D Gilbert, estate agent and photographer: papers 20th cent

Britannia Foundry: records 20th cent

Johnson Bros & Co Ltd, fencing mfrs: records 20th cent

Walsall & District Co-operative Society Ltd: further records 20th cent

South Staffordshire Aero Club: further records 20th cent

Walsall Chamber of Commerce records 20th cent

WOLVERHAMPTON BOROUGH ARCHIVES, CENTRAL LIBRARY, SNOW HILL, WOLVERHAMPTON WV1 3AX

Thomas Reay Wood of Bilston, cinema proprietor and local politician: papers 20th cent

Alfred Hinde Ltd, printers: records 1924–88

Nock & Joseland, auctioneers and estate agents: records 18th–20th cent

Edwin Preston Ltd, brass founders: records 19th–20th cent

John Shaw & Sons, Wolverhampton, Ltd, hardware mfrs, Jenks Bros Ltd, small tool mfrs, and Britool Ltd: records c1790–1960

Smith, Son & Wilkie, chartered accountants: records 19th–20th cent, incl Wolverhampton Butchers Hide, Fat, Skin & Wool Co, Queen Square Syndicate (Wolverhampton) and Stockless Anchor Co

St Peter's Collegiate School records 1851–67

Queen Victoria Nursing Institution records 1898–1948

National Union of Sheet Metal Workers, Coppersmiths, Heating and Domestic Engineers: Wolverhampton branch records 1834–1984

NORFOLK

NORFOLK RECORD OFFICE, CENTRAL LIBRARY, BETHEL STREET, NORWICH NR2 1NJ

Kett family of Brooke House: deeds and papers 16th–19th cent

Starling and Freeman families of Norwich: corresp and papers, incl some while in Italy 1846–51 and on the Norfolk Broads 1843–94

Edmund Newdigate, physician: Watton estate and misc papers 1735–75

William Wallace, rector of Thorpe Abbotts: diaries 1840, 1842

Hockwold estate papers c1820–39

Saham Toney deeds 1492–1606

Horstead inclosure agreement 1599

Wereham Hall and Ironhall in Wereham manors: further records 1517–1956

Coleman & Co Ltd, wine merchants, Norwich: records c1920–79

Narborough farm ledger 1887–93

AE Plumstead & Co Ltd, gas engineers, Norwich: records 1906–40

Woods, Sadd, Moore & Co Ltd, barley and seed merchants, Norwich: Loddon wherry trading ledger 1904–30

Parish records of Ashill, Brooke, Coltishall, Great Hautbois, Horstead and Loddon 16th–20th cent; Anmer church book, mainly malt stock accounts, 1522–57

Ingham and Stalham Baptist Churches: records c1814–1988

St John's Roman Catholic Cathedral, Norwich: working drawings of Sir George Gilbert Scott and John Oldrid Scott c1883–1910

Harleston Benevolent Society records 1822–1988

Hunstanton Convalescent Home Trust records 1876–1982

Flemish and Walloon community, Norwich: register of bonds etc 1583–1600

NORTHAMPTONSHIRE

NORTHAMPTONSHIRE RECORD OFFICE, DELAPRÉ ABBEY, LONDON ROAD, NORTHAMPTON NN4 9AW

Kingsthorpe manor: further records 1350–1705

Northampton borough: further records c1500–1978, incl copy of *liber customarum* c1500 and register of freemen from 1661

NORTHUMBERLAND

NORTHUMBERLAND RECORD OFFICE, MELTON PARK, NORTH GOSFORTH, NEWCASTLE UPON TYNE NE3 5QX

Gibb family, farmers, of Eachwick: deeds and papers 16th–19th cent

Smith family of Haughton Castle: account book 1780–1805 and S African diaries of Robert John Smith 1860–63

Swinburne family, baronets, of
Capheaton: further estate papers
19th–20th cent

Thompson family of East Bolton: papers
rel to the Innes-Ker family, Dukes of
Roxburghe and the Forster and Gray
families 18th–20th cent

Sir Francis Brandling MP, sheriff of
Northumberland: quietus roll 1626

W Percy Hedley (fl1923), antiquary:
papers rel to Northumberland families

B Wild, primitive Methodist minister:
circuit account book 1853–96

James Dixon, joiner and cartwright,
Molesden: records 1830–95

John Hall Sanderson, wine and spirit
merchant, Alnwick: records 1884–1938

Jasper Stephenson of Newbiggin Farm,
Blanchland: farming records
19th–20th cent

Society of Skinners and Glovers,
Hexham: guild minute book 1740–1967

Weavers Company, Morpeth:
admissions of freemen 1715–1829

Co-operative Party, Northumberland
Federation: executive committee minutes
1937–71

BERWICK UPON TWEED BRANCH
RECORD OFFICE, COUNCIL OFFICES,
WALLACE GREEN,
BERWICK UPON TWEED TD15 1ED

Grieve family of Ord House: papers
17th–20th cent

Berwick Salmon Fisheries plc: records
17th–20th cent

Berwick Harbour Commissioners
records 19th–20th cent

NOTTINGHAMSHIRE

NOTTINGHAMSHIRE ARCHIVES OFFICE,
COUNTY HOUSE, HIGH PAVEMENT,
NOTTINGHAM NG1 1HR

Foljambe family of Osberton: further
estate papers 18th–20th cent

Gillot family of Bingham: farm accounts
1839–1901

Keyworth Hall deeds 1566–1910

Dobson Park Industries plc: records of
predecessor companies c1890–1950, incl
Bar-Lock (1925) Co, typewriter mfrs
and John Jardine Ltd, lace machinery and
bobbin carriage mfrs, Nottingham

Greater Nottingham Co-operative
Society records 19th–20th cent

JB Lewis & Sons Ltd, hosiery mfrs,
Nottingham (addnl): Ilkeston Junction
works records 1913–77

WJ Price & Son, bakers, Beeston: records
1920–86

John Player & Son Ltd, tobacco mfrs,
Nottingham: further records 19th–20th
cent

John Beetham Shaw, architect,
Bingham: business papers c1870–1939

Trustee Savings Bank, Retford and
Worksop branches: records 1818–1975

Gordon Memorial Home for Destitute
Boys, Nottingham: records 1884–1985

National Union of Railwaymen,
Nottingham No 2 branch: records
20th cent

Tobacco Trade Travellers Association,
Nottingham and East Midlands branch:
records 1946–87

Council of Christians and Jews,
Nottingham branch: records 20th cent

Electrical Association for Women,
Nottingham branch: records 20th cent

English Sinfonia Association records
20th cent

OXFORDSHIRE

OXFORDSHIRE ARCHIVES, COUNTY
HALL, NEW ROAD, OXFORD OX1 1ND

Page-Turner family, baronets, of
Ambrosden: estate accounts 1781–1811

Thomas Rennell, dean of Winchester:
sermons 18th cent

HM Walton, Oxfordshire county
archivist: papers 20th cent

Adderbury manorial records
16th–20th cent

Bicester Gas, Coke & Coal Co records
19th–20th cent

Thame and Watlington Methodist
Circuit records 1742–1985

Hart's Charity, Watlington: records
1698–1930

SHROPSHIRE

SHROPSHIRE RECORD OFFICE,
SHIREHALL, ABBEY FOREGATE,
SHREWSBURY SY2 6ND

Alderson family: Condover farm
account books 1924–28

Bishop, More and Mytton families of
Shipton: deeds 1689–1953

Broughton family of Tunstall Hall and
Church family: deeds 1321–1836

Darby family of Coalbrookdale:
Leighton Buzzard, Beds, deeds
1718–1861

Edwards family of Ness Strange: further
family and estate papers 14th–20th cent,
incl reeve's account roll for Albrighton
1398–1402, 1405–06, 1415–16

Broome estate deeds 1788–1892

Morgans, solicitors, Ludlow: clients
papers, mainly deeds, 18th–20th cent

Alliance Assurance Co Ltd, Shrewsbury
branch: records 1890–1973

Cheshire Cheese Federation records
1923–67

Electrical Association for Women:
minutes of Bridgnorth, Ludlow and
Wellington 1946–83 and Shrewsbury
1953–86 branches

Social Democratic Party, Wrekin branch:
minutes 1981–88

SOMERSET

SOMERSET RECORD OFFICE, OBRIDGE
ROAD, TAUNTON TA2 7PU

Tudway family of Wells: further Antigua
estate papers 1758–1818

Weston-super-Mare and Worle
Turnpike Trust: minutes and accounts
1840–82

STAFFORDSHIRE

STAFFORDSHIRE RECORD OFFICE,
EASTGATE STREET, STAFFORD ST16 2LZ

Fleetwood family, baronets, of Calwich:
deeds and estate papers 1545–1863

Paget family, Marquesses of Anglesey
(addnl): household and estate papers
1780–1840 and plans of Beaudesert Hall
c1840–1909

Bannister & Thatcher Ltd, pharmacists,
Rugeley: records 1878–1968

Blythe Colour Works, Hanley: recipes
19th cent

George Salter & Co Ltd, scale mfrs,
West Bromwich: records c1850–1985

Martin Street United Reformed Church,
Stafford: further records c1798–1988

Mount Street United Reformed Church,
Stafford: records 1791–1987

National Union of Mineworkers,
Midlands area: further records 1957–79

Tunstall Amicable Society accounts
1810–83

Lichfield Conduit Lands Trust: further
records 17th–20th cent

SUFFOLK

Thellusson family, Barons Rendlesham
(addnl): family and estate papers
1611–1940

Thomas Martin, antiquary: account
book 1726–31

British Sugar plc: records of Ipswich
factory 1928–87

Leiston Industrial Co-operative Society
Ltd: further records 1898–1939

John Spore, shoemaker, Chediston:
accounts 1768–78

National Communications Union,
Martlesham branch: records 1930–78

Ipswich Constituency Liberal
Association records 1978–87

Upcher family of Sudbury: family and
estate papers 17th–20th cent

Lord Arlington: accounts for paving at
his London house 1671

HG Frost, builders, Bury St Edmunds:
records 1889–1973

Savory & Moore Ltd, chemists, Bury St
Edmunds: prescription books 1891–1981

Clare United Reformed Church records
1696–20th cent

Ancient Order of Foresters: Woolpit
court 1864–1937 and Mildenhall area
records 1958–83

Sons of Temperance, Stanton sub-
division: accounts 1889–1917

Sudbury Friendly Society records
1885–1961

Suggate family of Mutford: family and
estate papers 1659–1878

J Riches, Lowestoft pilot: accounts
1937–53

William Cleveland, fish merchants,
Lowestoft: family and business papers
c1790–1851

Small & Co Ltd, steamship owners,
Lowestoft: customs records 1903–40

S Swonnell & Sons Ltd, maltsters,
Oulton Broad: records 1901–37

Lowestoft harbour: refuge, arrivals and
sailings books 1940–48

SURREY

Colyear family, Earls of Portmore:
family and Surrey and London estate
papers 1800–91, incl corresp of Francis
Wishaw, surveyor, rel to the Weybridge
estate 1800–08

Locke-King family of Brooklands:
papers rel to Brooklands Automobile
Racing Club 1900–22

Kenneth George Farries, writer on the
history of windmills: papers 20th cent

George Harry Trench: diaries of travel in
Europe 1883–92, 1904–09, 1920–29

Tertius TB Watson (1889–1987),
physician: papers

SURREY RECORD OFFICE, GUILDFORD
MUNIMENT ROOM, CASTLE ARCH,
GUILDFORD GU1 3SX

JI Blackburn & Co, general engineers, Godalming: Catteshall mill air raid diaries 1939–44

Drummond Bros Ltd, machine tool mfrs, Guildford: records 1902–81

Archbishop Abbot's Hospital Manufactory, Guildford: account books 1676–1851

Thorncombe Military Hospital and Fund records 1911–87

Surrey Home Guard, 4th Bn, Section 1: records 1941–44

Peper Harow House: plans by Lancelot 'Capability' Brown c1750

EAST SUSSEX

EAST SUSSEX RECORD OFFICE, THE
MALTINGS, CASTLE PRECINCTS,
LEWES BN7 1YT

Ashburnham family, baronets, of Broomham: estate accounts 1908–76

Frewen family of Brickwall: further family and estate papers 17th–20th cent

Lamb family, baronets, of Beauport: deeds and papers 1680–1925

Lansdell family of Hastings: accounts 1810–1910

Stone, Barclay and Bell Irving families of Mayfield: deeds and papers 1591–1906

Alexander Roper Vidler (1899–1984), theologian: personal and family papers

Blaker, Son & Young, solicitors, Lewes: further clients papers 19th–20th cent

Dawes, Prentice & Herington, solicitors, Rye: further clients papers 19th–20th cent

Fitzhugh Gates, solicitors, Brighton: clients papers 17th–20th cent

RA Larkin & Bros Ltd, builders, Bexhill: accounts and plans 1922–82

Riches & Gray, architects, Bexhill: plans c1888–1959

Thomas Rickman, merchant, of Lewes: accounts 1785–87

George Young, builder, Ticehurst: day books 1862–1934

Northiam Unitarian Chapel records 1795–1916

Sussex Law Society records 1875–1953

Kemp Town Enclosures Management Committee, Brighton: minutes 1828–1942

WEST SUSSEX

WEST SUSSEX RECORD OFFICE, COUNTY
HALL, CHICHESTER PO19 1RN

Gorringe family of Kingston House (addnl): family papers 1718–1985, incl some rel to flying at Shoreham 1926–33

Charles Bennet, 1st Earl of Tankerville: inventories and estate accounts 1722–23

William Hall, excise officer, of East Grinstead: corresp and papers 1808–41

Court books for the manors of Prinsted 1685–1804 and Westbourne 1685–1862

National Union of Railwaymen: Horsham General Strike committee minutes 1926

Workers Educational Association, Bognor Regis branch: records 1927–70

Sussex militia: papers rel to Chichester depot 19th cent

TYNE AND WEAR

TYNE AND WEAR ARCHIVES SERVICE,
BLANDFORD HOUSE, WEST
BLANDFORD STREET,
NEWCASTLE UPON TYNE NE1 4JA

Thomas A Davidson, assistant magistrates clerk: diaries 1844–46

Captain Robert Jopling, shipping master, of Newcastle: journal 1851–58

Lt G Rutherford, RNVR: diary of service on HMS *Menestheus*, *Patroller* and *Agamemnon* 1943–46

Richard Welford (1836–1919), local historian: corresp and papers

Adamsez Ltd, sanitary ware mfrs, Newcastle: further records from 1916

Austin & Pickersgill Ltd, shipbuilders, Sunderland: further records from 1880

Thomas F Convery Enterprises Ltd, theatrical agents, Newcastle: records 1926–30

Great Northern Telegraph Co Ltd of Denmark: Newcastle station note books 1878–1935

Sir James Laing & Sons Ltd, shipbuilders, Sunderland: further records 19th–20th cent

Newcastle upon Tyne Company of Millers: minutes 1611–69 and admissions 1722–1927

Newcastle upon Tyne & Gateshead Gas Co: further records 1829–1961

Renwick, Wilton & Dobson Ltd, coal exporters and Prince, Tatham & Co, shipbrokers, Newcastle: financial records *c*1920–60

Joseph L Thompson & Sons Ltd, shipbuilders, Sunderland: further records 19th–20th cent

Stanton Croft & Co, solicitors, Newcastle: further records 18th–20th cent

Sunderland Dry Dock & Engineering Co: further records 19th–20th cent

Wallsend Slipway & Engineering Co: further records 19th–20th cent

Howard Street Presbyterian Church, North Shields: records 1760–1949

Northumberland Square Presbyterian Church, North Shields: records 1781–1972

Winlaton Independent Chapel records from 1830

National and Local Government Officers Association, North East provincial council: minutes 1937–77

Institute of Almoners, Newcastle region: minutes 1930–64

Newcastle upon Tyne Incorporated Law Society records 1826–1938

North East Coast Engineering Employers Association and Border Counties Engineering Employers Association: records from 1872

Royal College of Midwives, Newcastle branch: records *c*1950–70

Teetotal Society of North Shields: minutes 1837–42

Newcastle upon Tyne Liberal Club: further records from 1882

North East Society Co-operative Party, Newcastle north branch: minutes 1969–80

Washington Development Corporation: further records *c*1965–88

WARWICKSHIRE

WARWICK COUNTY RECORD OFFICE, PRIORY PARK, CAPE ROAD, WARWICK CV34 4JS

Bettridge family, agricultural engineers, of Wellesbourne Hastings: family papers 1857–1971

Bloxam family of Rugby and Lilley Smith family of Southam: corresp and misc papers 1790–1914

Webb family of Sherbourne: corresp 1725–85

Ralph Sheldon of Weston Park: account book 1586–88

Michael Thompson, farmer, of Polesworth: rent receipt book 1740–93

DA Fyfe & Co Ltd, forage merchants, London: commercial traveller's Midlands letter book 1922–26

N Hawkes and H Bloomer, architects, Henley-in-Arden: working papers rel to Warwicks churches 1960–85

Leamington Spa Building Society records 1853–1972

Ancient Order of Druids, Austrey lodge: records 1844–1908

Independent Order of Oddfellows, Earl of Warwick and Percy lodges: records 1843–1921

Corbett family of Admington Hall: deeds 1736–1929

David Garrick, actor: papers rel to his loans 1777

Selina Flower (d1883): commonplace book

Stratford-upon-Avon to Moreton-in-Marsh tramway: clerk's letter book 1845–47

ISLE OF WIGHT

John M Morris of Yarmouth: yachting log books 1968–82

Carisbrooke Priory manor court book 1730–82

NM Richley, mortgage brokers, Shanklin: Newport deeds 1814–1924

Robinson, Jarvis & Rolf, solicitors, Ryde: deeds and papers 1861–1934

Leigh Thomas & Co Ltd, provender millers and grain merchants, Newport: Pan Mills deeds 1787–1921

Cowes Chamber of Trade: minutes 1947–73

WILTSHIRE

H Bevir & Son, solicitors, Wootton Bassett: family and estate papers of the St John family, Viscounts Bolingbroke 18th–20th cent

Phelps & Lawrence, solicitors, Ramsbury: further records 18th–20th cent, incl Somerset Hospital, Froxfield estate maps

Ben Nevis Packaging Ltd, packaging machinery mfrs, Trowbridge: records c1940–88

Cow & Gate Ltd, baby food mfrs, Trowbridge: records c1900–88

HR & S Sainsbury Ltd, agricultural merchants, Trowbridge: records 1930–76

Usher's Wiltshire Brewery Ltd, Trowbridge: further records 19th–20th cent

TH White Ltd, agricultural engineers, Devizes: records 1876–1987

Society of Wiltshire Archers records 1853–1987

Transferred from Swindon Public L

Goddard family of Swindon: family and estate papers 1346–20th cent

Wilts & Berks Canal Co: records 1793–1914

NORTH YORKSHIRE

Farsyde family of Fylingdales: family papers 1735–1870

William Oliver: local history collections

Cropton manor court papers 1685–1777 and Pickering estate and parish records 1412–18th cent, incl court of survey records 17th cent

Yorkshire Agricultural Society minutes
1837–1947

Scarborough shipping registers
1786–1918

Fairbank & Son, civil engineers: records
c1850–1970

SOUTH YORKSHIRE

Wilson Waring, stud and chaplet maker:
diaries and papers 1900–39

Wilson & Longbottom Ltd, loom
makers: records c1875–1976

National Union of Mineworkers, Elsecar
Main Colliery branch: records c1933–53

Electrical Association for Women,
Barnsley branch: records 1981–85

Independent Order of Rechabites,
Barnsley branch no 88: records
c1870–1940

Hunshelf township records 1740–1950,
incl inclosure award and plan 1813

Royston survey and rate book 1824

Clark family of Doncaster: further deeds
and papers 1611–1921

Trustee Savings Bank: records of Balby
1945–76 and Thorne 1939–75 branches

Amalgamated Union of Engineering
Workers, Doncaster no 7 branch: records
1949–87

National Council on Inland Transport:
corresp 1963–86

Electrical Association for Women:
minute books of Doncaster 1972–85 and
Thorne 1965–77 branches

Railway Development Society, London
area: secretary's corresp 1963–84

Thomas Newbould, mining engineer:
diaries and papers c1820–1920

Parker, Rhodes, Burgess & Co,
solicitors: further clients and practice
papers 15th–20th cent, incl manor court
records for Dalton 15th cent and
Rawmarsh 17th cent

Beatson, Clark & Co Ltd, glass container
mfrs: records 18th–20th cent

Dale, Brown & Co, glass bottle mfrs,
Swinton: further records c1918–88

David B and ADP Jenkinson, architects:
records 1892–1982

Drabble family: corresp 1841–49

David Blunkett (b1947) MP: papers

Richard George Caborn (b1943) MP:
papers

Edward Carpenter, author: further
corresp 1888–1925

Cortonwood Collieries Co Ltd,
Wombwell (addnl): time books and
diaries 20th cent

Benjamin Huntsman Ltd, steel mfrs:
further records c1870–1900

J Preston Ltd, laboratory furnishers:
records c1850–1950

Roberts & Belk Ltd, silver platers and
cutlers: further records 19th–20th cent

Joseph Rodgers & Sons Ltd, cutlers: further records 19th–20th cent

F Tory & Sons, architectural sculptors: records 1904–67

Trustee Savings Bank, Norfolk Street branch: records 1819–1974

Amalgamated Union of Engineering Workers, Hillsborough branch: minutes 1958–73

Geographical Association records c1893–1988

Campaign for Nuclear Disarmament, Sheffield branch: minutes 1963–67

Airedale Co-operative Society Ltd: further records c1860–1985

Sydney Packett & Sons, insurance brokers: business registers 1945–83

Leonard Stead & Son Ltd, plaster mfrs: records c1930–79

Julius Whitehead & Son, builders merchants: records c1892–1972

Chapel Lane Unitarian Chapel, Bradford: records 1719–1967

Queensbury Baptist Chapel, Bradford: records c1748–1928

Bradford Historical and Antiquarian Society records 1878–1967

WEST YORKSHIRE

WEST YORKSHIRE ARCHIVE SERVICE HEADQUARTERS, REGISTRY OF DEEDS, NEWSTEAD ROAD, WAKEFIELD WF1 2DE

Fennel, White and Tolson families of Wakefield: family papers 19th–20th cent

Thomas Pumphrey (1802–62), superintendent of Ackworth School: papers, with those of his wife Rachel

Joseph Sharp, Yorkshire emigrant to the USA: papers 1811–28

Horbury Common Lands Trust: further records 1817–1982

National and Local Government Officers Association, West Yorkshire branch: records 1974–86

National Union of Teachers, Castleford, Pontefract and District Association: records 1930–87

WEST YORKSHIRE ARCHIVE SERVICE, BRADFORD DISTRICT ARCHIVES, 15 CANAL ROAD, BRADFORD BD1 4AT

Spencer Stanhope family of Cannon Hall: further family and estate papers 18th cent

Joseph Horsfall Turner, antiquary: papers rel to local biography c1890–1914

Transferred from Bradford Univ L

FH Bentham Ltd, wool comb makers: records 1859–1944

Cleckheaton Industrial Co-operative Society Ltd: further records 1855–1973

Bradford Sanitary Association records 1881–1923

Bradford Typographical Society records 1854–1969

Worsted Committee of Yorkshire, Lancashire and Chester: records 1777–1951

WEST YORKSHIRE ARCHIVE SERVICE, CALDERDALE DISTRICT ARCHIVES, CENTRAL LIBRARY, NORTHGATE HOUSE, HALIFAX HX1 1UN

Fielden family of Langfield: deeds and papers 1603–1943

Radcliffe family, baronets, of Rudding Park: deeds 1620–1834

Greenwood Stell & Sons Ltd, textile mfrs, Mytholmroyd and Central Dyeing Co Ltd, fustian dyers, Heptonstall: records 1909–80

Carlton United Reformed Church, Halifax: records 1836–1970

Eastwood Congregational Church
records 1693–1963

Elland and Greetland Methodist Circuit:
further records 1810–1980

Providence United Reformed Church,
Ovenden: records 1836–1978

Calder Valley Conservative Association
records 1887–1974

Transferred from Bradford Univ L

Baldwin & Walker Ltd, knitting wool
mfrs, Halifax: records 1836–1974

I & I Calvert Ltd, worsted spinners,
Halifax: records 1637–1968

WEST YORKSHIRE ARCHIVE SERVICE,
KIRKLEES DISTRICT ARCHIVES,
CENTRAL LIBRARY, PRINCESS
ALEXANDRA WALK,
HUDDERSFIELD HD1 2SU

Florence E Lockwood, Black Rock
Mills, Linthwaite: war diary and notes
1914–18

Crosland & Fenton, solicitors,
Huddersfield: further clients papers
1441–1910

Brierley Bros Ltd, woollen yarn
spinners, Huddersfield: financial records
1883–1965

Almondbury Grammar School and
Wormall's Charity: records 1609–1950

Assistant Masters Association,
Huddersfield sub-branch: minutes
1920–73

Huddersfield and District
Chrysanthemum Society records
1884–1987

Union Discussion Society, Huddersfield:
records 1871–1968

Tolson Museum MS collections:
township, business, family, personal and
estate papers 16th–20th cent

WEST YORKSHIRE ARCHIVE SERVICE,
LEEDS DISTRICT ARCHIVES,
CHAPELTOWN ROAD, SHEEPSCAR,
LEEDS LS7 3AP

Lane Fox family of Bramham Park:
further estate papers 1815–43

William Radford Bilbrough:
diaries 1852–1906

J Town: diaries 1827–55

Cranswick Watson, solicitors: clients
papers 18th–19th cent

John Hainsworth & Sons Ltd, woollen
mfrs, Farsley: records 19th–20th cent

EJ Rawlins & Co Ltd, paint mfrs:
records 20th cent

Kippax St Mary parish (addnl): registers
1536–1969

Order of Ancient Maccabeans, Mount
Sinai Beacon No 8 (Brunswick Street,
Leeds): records 1933–70

Seacroft and Crossgates Cycling Club
records 1898–1984

WEST YORKSHIRE ARCHIVE SERVICE,
YORKSHIRE ARCHAEOLOGICAL
SOCIETY, CLAREMONT, 23 CLARENDON
ROAD, LEEDS LS2 9NZ

RG Rowley: deeds and papers rel to the
Skipton area 17th–20th cent

Leeds Freemasons, Leeds chapter, Rose
Croix No 77: records 1878–1987

Local Repositories: Wales

CLWYD

CLWYD RECORD OFFICE,
THE OLD RECTORY,
HAWARDEN, DEESIDE CH5 3NR

Mostyn family, Barons Mostyn: further
Flints and Llandudno estate papers
18th–20th cent

Stephen Barry Jones MP: papers rel to
closure of Shotton steelworks 1975–78

Catherall & Co Ltd, brick and tile mfrs,
Buckley: further records c1947–80

Holywell-Halkyn Mining & Tunnel Co
(addnl): plans and sections of Flints and
Denbighs lead mines 19th–20th cent

National and Local Government Officers
Association, Flintshire county branch:
records 1938–73

Flintshire Beekeepers Association:
minutes 1956–76

Rhyl Golf Club: minutes 1890–96

CLWYD RECORD OFFICE,
46 CLWYD STREET, RUTHIN LL15 1HP

David Swynford Foulkes-Roberts
(1899–1988), teacher and administrator
in Nigeria: diaries

Nott's, stationers, Denbigh: ledger
1903–12

L Rowland & Co, chemists, Wrexham:
records c1800–1986

Swan Lane Independent Chapel,
Denbigh: records 1763–1951

William and John Jones Charity,
Wrexham: records c1817–1970

Plaid Cymru, Abergele branch: records
1976–84

2nd Bn Denbighshire Home Guard:
records 1940–45

DYFED

DYFED ARCHIVE SERVICE,
CARMARTHENSHIRE RECORD OFFICE,
COUNTY HALL, CARMARTHEN SA31 1JP

Campbell family, Earls Cawdor:
further map books of Golden Grove
demesne 1794 and other
Carmarthenshire estates 1795

Llwynywormwood estate rentals
1843–67

Carmarthen and Dyfed Liberal
Association records 1960–80

DYFED ARCHIVE SERVICE,
CARDIGANSHIRE RECORD OFFICE,
COUNTY OFFICE, MARINE TERRACE,
ABERYSTWYTH SY23 2DE

Jonathan Evans, postmaster, Cardigan:
family papers 1824–1924

Lovesgrove estate papers 1812–1912

Graham Davies, Kevin Williams & Co,
solicitors, Lampeter: deeds and papers
1756–1962

DYFED ARCHIVE SERVICE,
PEMBROKESHIRE RECORD OFFICE, THE
CASTLE, HAVERFORDWEST SA61 2EF

Eaton-Evans & Morris, solicitors,
Haverfordwest: further deeds and papers
17th–19th cent

VJG Johns & Son, solicitors, Fishguard:
deeds and papers 18th–20th cent

James John & Sons, ironmongers,
Narberth: records 1856–1949

GLAMORGAN (MID, SOUTH AND WEST)

GLAMORGAN ARCHIVE SERVICE,
GLAMORGAN RECORD OFFICE,
COUNTY HALL, CATHAYS PARK,
CARDIFF CF1 3NE

Kemeys-Tynte family of Cefn Mably:
further deeds 1341–1850

Lewis family of New House: deeds and
papers 1649–1924

Lewis family of Penmark: deeds and
papers 1684–1710

Stockwood family of Bridgend: further
papers 20th cent

Cynon Colliery Co Ltd, Port Talbot:
records 20th cent

Glamorgan Wagon Co Ltd, rolling stock
financiers, Cardiff: records 1913–73

North's Navigation Collieries (1889)
Ltd, Cardiff: further records 20th cent

Powell Duffryn Steam Coal Co Ltd,
Cardiff: further records 19th–20th cent

Reardon Smith Line Ltd, shipowners,
Cardiff: records 1914–83

Welsh Associated Collieries Ltd, Cardiff:
records 20th cent

National Union of Railwaymen,
Llantrisant branch: registers 1875–1972
and minutes 1925–82

GLAMORGAN ARCHIVE SERVICE, WEST
GLAMORGAN AREA RECORD OFFICE,
COUNTY HALL, OYSTERMOUTH ROAD,
SWANSEA SA1 3SN

Registry of Shipping and Seamen:
seamen's record cards 19th–20th cent

GWENT

GWENT RECORD OFFICE, COUNTY HALL,
CWMBRAN NP44 2XH

Bridge Farm, Llanfihangel Crucorney:
deeds 1801–1938

Newport deeds 19th–20th cent

John Basham & Sons, nurserymen and
florists, Bassaleg: accounts 1896–1930

Ford & Moore Ltd, ironmongers,
Newport: journals and wage books
1935–70

T Hewertson & Co, wholesale
tobacconists, Newport: accounts
1874–1987

AJ Jacobs & Sons, pawnbrokers,
Newport: accounts 1914–49

Socialist Education Association, South
Wales branch: minutes 1973–85

Newport Pilotage Authority: further
records 19th–20th cent

GWYNEDD

GWYNEDD ARCHIVES SERVICE,
CAERNARFON AREA RECORD OFFICE,
COUNTY OFFICES,
CAERNARFON LL55 1SH

Owen Parry, chemist and optician,
Portmadoc: records 1893–1964

James George Tuxford, roofing
contractor, Conway: records 20th cent

F Tyldesley Ltd, builders and
contractors, Llandudno: records
c1940–79

Evan Williams, saddler, Tremadoc:
ledgers, incl some of his predecessor
William Williams, 1861–1958

Independent Broadcasting Authority,
North and West Wales area: papers rel to
transmitting stations 1960–88

GWYNEDD ARCHIVES SERVICE,
DOLGELLAU AREA RECORD OFFICE,
CAE PENARLAG, DOLGELLAU LL40 2YB

Elwyn Roberts (d1988), treasurer of
Plaid Cymru: family and political papers

Madoc Granite Quarry Co, Blaenau
Ffestiniog: records 20th cent

North Wales Quarrymens Union,
Ffestiniog branch: minutes 1920–55

GWYNEDD ARCHIVES SERVICE,
LLANGEFNI AREA RECORD OFFICE,
SHIRE HALL, LLANGEFNI LL77 7TW

Owen family of Llanfairpwll: corresp
late 19th–20th cent

Trescawen estate, Llangwyllog: deeds
and papers 1685–1935

Owen Jones, butcher and grocer, Menai
Bridge: ledgers and day book 1872–1963

JH Moss, grocer, Menai Bridge: account
books and ledgers 20th cent

POWYS

POWYS ARCHIVES, LIBRARIES AND
MUSEUMS DEPARTMENT,
CEFNLLYS ROAD,
LLANDRINDOD WELLS LD1 5LD

Bonnor-Maurice family of Bodynfoel:
family and estate papers 1532–1921

Sandbach family of Hafodunos and
Bryngwyn: family and estate papers
c1800–1930, incl papers of Major-
General Arthur Edmund Sandbach
(1859–1928)

Llansanffraid Cwmteuddwr: deeds
1702–63

Presteigne deeds and maps 1730–1833

Tregoed, Glasbury: deeds 1623–1975

Society of Friends: Pales Meeting House,
Llandegley, records 1673–1855

Local Repositories: Scotland

CENTRAL

CENTRAL REGIONAL COUNCIL
ARCHIVES DEPARTMENT, UNIT 6,
BURGHMUIR INDUSTRIAL ESTATE,
STIRLING FK7 7PY

Clan Gregor Society records 1822–1985

DUMFRIES AND GALLOWAY

DUMFRIES ARCHIVE CENTRE,
33 BURNS STREET, DUMFRIES DG1 2PS

Clerk-Maxwell family of Middlebie:
family and estate papers 1630–1920

McCartney family of Halketleaths:
family and legal papers 1566–1835

William McBryde: diary of voyage to
Queensland 1862

Knockvennie Smithy, blacksmiths: day
books 1855–1911

Moffat Gas Light Co Ltd: register
1884–98

Maxwelltown Relief Church records
1809–79

GRAMPIAN

CITY OF ABERDEEN DISTRICT
ARCHIVES, THE CHARTER ROOM, THE
TOWN HOUSE, ABERDEEN AB9 1AQ

Robert Gordon's Institute of
Technology: hospital and college records
c1740–1940, incl Gray's School of Arts
and Crafts

George Donald & Sons Ltd, glass, paint
and wallpaper merchants: records
1845–1970

Aberdeen Soup Kitchen minutes and
accounts 1828–1928

Transferred from Grampian Regional Archives

Farquhar & Gill, paint, oil and wallpaper mfrs: records 19th–20th cent

John Fyfe Ltd, quarry owners and granite merchants: records 19th–20th cent

Rubislaw Granite Co Ltd, quarry proprietors and merchants: records 19th–20th cent

LOTHIAN

CITY OF EDINBURGH DISTRICT COUNCIL ARCHIVES, DEPARTMENT OF ADMINISTRATION, CITY CHAMBERS, HIGH STREET, EDINBURGH EH1 1YJ

Thomas Elder, lord provost: letter book 1767–84

Brown Brothers & Co Ltd: Rosebank ironworks records 1890–1905

STRATHCLYDE

STRATHCLYDE REGIONAL ARCHIVES, MITCHELL LIBRARY, 201 NORTH STREET, GLASGOW G3 7DN

Barns-Graham family of Lymekilns: deeds 16th–19th cent

Crum family of Thornliebank: corresp 19th–20th cent

Montgomerie Flemings, Fyfe, Maclean & Co, solicitors, Glasgow (addnl): trust records 19th–20th cent

Coltness Iron Co Ltd, Newmains: records 17th–20th cent

Western Scottish Motor Transport Co Ltd, Kilmarnock: financial records 1904–81

Thomas Coates Memorial Church (Baptist), Paisley: records 1788–1973

Scottish Co-operative Womens Guild: records 1892–1984

West of Scotland Bible Society minutes 1848–68

Glasgow Co-operative Party records 1917–86

ARGYLL AND BUTE DISTRICT ARCHIVES, KILMORY, LOCHGILPHEAD PA31 8RT

Campbell family of Ormidale: papers 1778–1905

Campbeltown Coal Co Ltd: records 1900–28

Argyll and the Isles Episcopal diocese: records 1847–20th cent

Scottish Rural Workers Approved Society, Knapdale branch: records 1929–41

TAYSIDE

DUNDEE DISTRICT ARCHIVE AND RECORD CENTRE, CITY CHAMBERS, CITY SQUARE, DUNDEE DD1 3BY

Bell & Sime, timber importers and sawmillers, Dundee: records 1888–1980

Arbroath Congregational Church: further records 1834–1934

PERTH AND KINROSS DISTRICT ARCHIVE, SANDEMAN LIBRARY, 16 KINNOULL STREET, PERTH PH1 5ET

Moir and Drummond families of Auchterarder: deeds and papers 1477–1900

Speid family of Forneth: estate papers c1846–1910

Valentine's Motors Ltd, Perth: further records 1921–84

William Stewart's Trust, Perth: minutes 1814–1902

Young Mens Christian Association. Alyth branch: records 1919–61

Baker Incorporation of Perth: records 1652–1973

II: Reports added to the National Register of Archives

The list notices Reports Nos 30611 to 31668 added to the National Register of Archives in 1988.

Appended is a short supplementary list of some of the more significant replacements and additions to existing reports received during the year.

Asterisks denote reports of which copies have also been sent to the British Library (Official Publications Library), the Bodleian Library Oxford, the University Library Cambridge, London University Institute of Historical Research, The John Rylands University Library of Manchester, The National Library of Scotland, The Scottish Record Office, The National Library of Wales and the Public Record Office of Northern Ireland.

Nos 30611–31668

30611 Rupert Hugh Morris, canon of St Davids: historical corresp and papers 16pp *Chester City RO*

30612 Chester Soroptimist International Club 4pp *Chester City RO*

30613 City of Westminster board of guardians 106pp *Greater London RO*

30614 W Evans George & Sons, solicitors, Newcastle Emlyn: clients papers 463pp *National L of Wales*

30615 Llanelly Savings Bank 2pp *Glamorgan RO*

30616 Sir Hugh Dow, Indian civil servant: corresp and papers 4pp *India Office L*

30617 Indian Political Service Collection 8pp *India Office L*

30618 Hull Seamens and General Orphanage 36pp *Hull City RO*

30619 Long family of Hurts Hall: family and estate papers 4pp *Suffolk RO, Ipswich*

30620 Middlesex County Association and London Diocesan Guild of Church Bell Ringers 7pp *Greater London RO*

30621 Henniker-Major family, Barons Henniker: family and estate papers 9pp *Suffolk RO, Ipswich*

30622 Bateman-Hanbury family, Barons Bateman: family and estate papers 5pp *Suffolk RO, Ipswich*

30623 Barrington family, Viscounts Barrington: family and official corresp and papers 12pp *Suffolk RO, Ipswich*

30624 Chard Borough 27pp *Somerset RO*

30625 Wells: Blue Coat School 12pp *Somerset RO*

30626 Mackay family of Bighouse, Sutherland: family and estate papers 34pp *Scottish RO*

30627 John Mackay, solicitor, Edinburgh: autograph collection 27pp *Scottish RO*

30628 Urquhart deeds and papers 23pp *Scottish RO*

30629 Society in Scotland for Propagating Christian Knowledge 41pp *Scottish RO*

30630 Sinclair family, Earls of Caithness: family and estate papers 113pp *Scottish RO*

30631 Richard Colley Wellesley, Marquess Wellesley and Richard Wellesley MP: family and personal papers 31pp *Southampton Univ L*

30632 Lewis Lloyd of Nantgwyllt, Radnor: estate and family papers 178pp *Powys Archives*

30633 British Federation of University Women: Cambridge branch 4pp *Cambs RO, Cambridge*

30634 John Heathcoat & Co Ltd, lace and textile mfrs, Tiverton 12pp *Devon RO and Tiverton Mus, Devon*

30635 Hulse family, baronets, of Breamore: family and estate papers 200pp *Private*

30636 Gardiner family, baronets, of Roche Court: deeds and estate papers 47pp *Hants RO*

30637 Union of Speech Therapists 1p *Warwick University Modern Records Centre*

30638 Perth: Guildry Incorporation 4pp *Private*

30639 Thomas Ferguson Rodger, professor of psychological medicine: corresp and papers 57pp *Glasgow Univ Archives*

30640 Charles William Bannister, botanist: journals and notebooks 4pp *Glos RO*

30641 Tewkesbury United Reformed Church 1p *Glos RO*

30642 Berry Hill: Salem Free Church 1p *Glos RO*

30643 Heatherbank Museum of Social Work, Glasgow: MS collections 6pp *Heatherbank Mus of Social Work, Glasgow*

30644 Anderson, Fyfe, Stewart & Young, solicitors, Glasgow 30pp *Strathclyde Regional Archives*

30645 Macrae, Flett & Rennie, solicitors, Edinburgh: clients papers 9pp *St Andrews Univ L*

30646 Commercial Friendly Society of Scotland and Glasgow Sailors Home 7pp *Strathclyde Regional Archives*

30647 Glasgow: Downanhill Church 3pp *Strathclyde Regional Archives*

30648 Glasgow: Weavers Society of Anderston 4pp *Strathclyde Regional Archives*

30649 Thomas Stewart Ltd, building contractors, Battlefield, Glasgow and Edinburgh 3pp *Strathclyde Regional Archives*

30650 Glasgow and Clyde Ship Owners Association 5pp *Strathclyde Regional Archives*

30651 Airdrie and Coatbridge Methodist Circuit 9pp *Strathclyde Regional Archives*

30652 Ferguson & Forrestor, restauranteurs, Glasgow 9pp *Strathclyde Regional Archives*

30653 Scottish Band of Hope Union 5pp *Strathclyde Regional Archives*

30654 Glasgow: Arlington Baths Club 9pp *Strathclyde Regional Archives*

30655 John Y Robertson & Co, solicitors, Hamilton, Lanarkshire: clients papers 9pp *Strathclyde Regional Archives*

30656 GJ Mason & Co Ltd, mantle mfrs, Glasgow 5pp *Strathclyde Regional Archives*

30657 George Thomson, professor of chemistry, Glasgow University: historical corresp and papers 20pp *Strathclyde Regional Archives*

30658 Glasgow Unitarian Church 4pp *Strathclyde Regional Archives*

30659 British Dyewood Co Ltd, Glasgow 3pp *Strathclyde Regional Archives*

30660 John Hardie & Co, shipowners and managers, Glasgow 11pp *Strathclyde Regional Archives*

30661 Glasgow: Western Amateur Swimming Club and Humane Society 3pp *Strathclyde Regional Archives*

30662 Glasgow: Victoria Infirmary Dorcas Society 4pp *Strathclyde Regional Archives*

30663 H Hogarth & Sons Ltd, shipowners, Glasgow 6pp *Strathclyde Regional Archives*

30664 Martin–Black plc, wire rope mfrs, Coatbridge 13pp *Strathclyde Regional Archives*

30665 Liberal Party: Glasgow Hillhead association 3pp *Strathclyde Regional Archives*

30666 Alfred Mylne & Co, marine architects, Glasgow 20pp *Strathclyde Regional Archives*

30667 Sir Robert Muir, pathologist: corresp and papers 8pp *Glasgow Univ Archives*

30668 George Maclean, missionary: corresp and papers 10pp *Glasgow Univ Archives*

30669 John Smith, geologist and naturalist: notebooks 6pp *Glasgow Univ Archives*

30670 Alexander John Haddow, professor of administrative medicine: corresp and papers 11pp *Glasgow Univ Archives*

30671 George William Barrington, 7th Viscount Barrington: corresp and papers 3pp *Duke Univ L, Durham, N Carolina, USA*

30672 Toy Town Shoes Ltd, Leicester 10pp *Leics RO*

30673 Liberty Shoe Co, footwear mfrs, Leicester 7pp *Leics RO*

30674 John B Jackson Ltd, jeweller, Southsea 9pp *Portsmouth City RO*

30675 National Union of Dyers, Bleachers and Textile Workers: Greetland branch 10pp *Calderdale District Archives*

*30676 Claude Gordon Douglas, physiologist: corresp and papers 30pp *History of Neuroscience L, Oxford*

30677 Colwyn Bay and Llandudno Methodist Circuit 6pp *Gwynedd Archives Service, Caernarfon*

30678 Glasgow: Trinity College 11pp *Glasgow Univ Archives*

30679 Edinburgh Soroptimist International Club 14pp *Edinburgh District Archives*

30680 Robert Simpson Silver, professor of mechanical engineering: corresp and papers 70pp *Glasgow Univ Archives*

30681 John Macdonald & Co (Pneumatic Tools)Ltd, East Kilbride 6pp *Private*

30682 Patrick Campbell, Church of Scotland minister: personal and family corresp and papers 9pp *Argyll and Bute District Archives*

30683 Council of Christian and Jews 17pp *Southampton Univ L*

30684 Douglas family, Earls of Morton: deeds and estate papers 17pp *Scottish RO*

30685 William Wynn Simpson, secretary of the International Council of Christians and Jews: corresp and papers 5pp *Southampton Univ L*

30686 Sir William Macewen, surgeon, and James W Allan, physician: corresp and papers 30pp *Glasgow Univ Archives*

30687 John Lorne Campbell, author and folklorist: Argyllshire deeds and papers 53pp *Scottish RO*

30688 William Wilson Saunders, naturalist: journals and family corresp 6pp *Bucks RO*

30689 Labour Party: Amersham branch 4pp *Bucks RO*

30690 Royal South Bucks Agricultural Association 3pp *Bucks RO*

30691 WJ Markham & Son, ironmongers, Buckingham 2pp *Bucks RO*

30692 Conservative Party: Beaconsfield constituency 3pp *Bucks RO*

30693 Bird Brothers, builders and contractors, Milton Keynes 3pp *Bucks RO*

30694 T Grace & Sons, builders, Quainton 4pp *Bucks RO*

30695 James Fraser, bishop of Manchester: papers 2pp *Chethams L, Manchester*

30696 Edward Bradley, novelist: corresp papers 98pp *Durham Univ L*

30697 Thomas Hogg, land agent to Durham dean and chapter: corresp and papers 19pp *Durham Univ L*

30698 Cumnock and Doon Valley District Library: MS collection 18pp *Various locations*

30699 D Gurteen & Sons Ltd, clothing and mat mfrs, Haverhill 12pp *Private*

30700 Joseph Cowen, politician and journalist: corresp and papers 463pp *Tyne and Wear Archives Dept*

30701 Hearsey family: corresp and and papers mainly rel to India 33pp *National Army Mus*

30702 Crewe Memorial Cottage Hospital 4pp *Cheshire RO*

30703 Nantwich Joint Hospital Board 2pp *Cheshire RO*

30704 Nantwich and District Cottage Hospital 1p *Cheshire RO*

30705 Birkenhead & District Co-operative Society 3pp *Wirral Archives*

30706 Birkenhead and Wirral Invalid Childrens Association 2pp *Wirral Archives*

30707 William Henry Ellis, solicitor, Llanfairfechan, Caerns: family and business corresp and papers 41pp *Gwynedd Archives Service, Caernarfon*

30708 Abraham Foulkes, surveyor, Newbridge, Denbighs 34pp *Gwynedd Archives Service, Caernarfon*

30709 Bangor, Caerns: Friars School 65pp *Gwynedd Archives Service, Caernarfon*

30710 Garlandstone Maritime Museum, Porthmadog, Caerns: MS collection 141pp *Gwynedd Archives Service, Caernarfon*

30711 Griffith Hughes, Calvinistic methodist minister: family corresp and papers 77pp *Gwynedd Archives Service, Caernarfon*

30712 Platt family of Gorddinog, Caerns: family and estate papers 139pp *Gwynedd Archives Service, Caernarfon*

30713 Cwmbran: Fairhill Methodist and Anglican Shared Church 11pp *Gwent RO*

30714 Gwent Methodist Circuit 6pp *Gwent RO*

30715 Chepstow: Beulah Independent Chapel 4pp *Gwent RO*

30716 Tredegar: Park Place Presbyterian Church 2pp *Gwent RO*

30717 WH Brakspear & Sons Ltd, brewers, Henley-on-Thames 4pp *Oxon RO*

30718 Ebbw Vale: Penuel Calvinistic Methodist Chapel 1p *Gwent RO*

30719 Monmouth: Glendower Street Congregational Church 1p *Gwent RO*

30720 Edinburgh District Archives: misc accessions 5pp *Edinburgh District Archives*

30721 Grimsby Steam and Diesel Fishing Vessels Engineers and Firemans Union 3pp *Warwick University Modern Records Centre*

30722 Ponthir: Zion Baptist Church 2pp *Gwent RO*

30723 Conolly family of Castletown: family and estate papers 4pp *Private*

30724 Lefroy family of Carrigglas Manor: family and estate papers 200pp *Private*

30725 Brudenell-Bruce family, Marquesses of Ailesbury: family and estate papers 520pp *Wilts RO and Private*

30726 Yorkshire Catholic Apolistic churches 4pp *Borthwick Inst, York*

30727 Church of England Mens Society: York diocesan union 3pp *Borthwick Inst, York*

30728 Sunbury Urban District Council 33pp *Greater London RO*

30729 Chepstow Water Co and Gwent Water Board 5pp *Gwent RO*

30730 Berry Bros & Rudd Ltd, wine and spirit merchants, London 17pp *Private*

30731 Wirral District Football Association 2pp *Wirral Archives*

30732 Newcastle upon Tyne: Wansbeck Home for Penitent Women 6pp *Tyne and Wear Archives Dept*

30733 Sunderland: West Park United Reformed Church 12pp *Tyne and Wear Archives Dept*

30734 Sunderland: Willmore Street United Reformed Church 5pp *Tyne and Wear Archives Dept*

30735 Sir John Sherburn: Whitburn and Cleadon, Co Durham, estate papers 18pp *Tyne and Wear Archives Dept*

30736 Rhodes Bros Sons Ltd, shetland shawl mfrs, Hucknall 2pp *Notts RO*

30737 Miller & Co, linen and woollen drapers, Sutton in Ashfield 2pp *Notts RO*

30738 JH Wilford (Nottingham) Ltd, lace mfrs 1p *Notts RO*

30739 Robert Francis Brown & Co Ltd, lace merchants, Nottingham 4pp *Notts RO*

30740 Chard Lace Co Ltd, lace and plain net mfrs, Nottingham 5pp *Notts RO*

30741 Thomas Adams Ltd, lace mfrs, Nottingham 4pp *Notts RO*

30742 Dublin: South City Markets Fire Relief Fund 75pp *Dublin Public L*

30743 Westminster: Hinde Street Methodist Circuit 12pp *Westminster Archives Dept, Marylebone*

30744 Southampton City Museums Archaeological Society 3pp *Southampton City RO*

30745 William Aspinall, decorators merchant, Burnley 1p *Burnley Central L, Lancs*

30746 Benjamin Thornber & Sons Ltd, cotton spinners and mfrs, Burnley 4pp *Burnley Central L, Lancs*

30747 Richard Hargreaves & Sons Ltd, tea merchants, Burnley 9pp *Burnley Central L, Lancs*

30748 Hargreaves (Executors Of John) Ltd, coal proprietors and merchants, Burnley 3pp *Burnley Central L, Lancs*

30749 Charity Commission: Monmouthshire charities accounts 27pp *Gwent RO*

30750 Liverpool: Fountains Road Synagogue 1p *Liverpool RO*

30751 Liverpool: Greenbank Drive Synagogue 10pp *Liverpool RO and Private*

30752 Liverpool: Nusach Ari Synagogue 1p *Liverpool RO*

30753 Liverpool Old Hebrew Congregation 20pp *Liverpool RO and Private*

30754 Liverpool Progressive Synagogue 1p *Liverpool RO*

30755 Barné of Sotterley and Dunwich: family and estate papers 97pp *Suffolk RO, Ipswich*

30756 Sir Hugh Carleton Greene, director-general of the BBC: corresp and papers 5pp *Private*

30757 Woolwich Group Hospital Management Committee 4pp *Greater London RO*

30758 Olivia Truman, author: corresp and misc papers 2pp *Bristol Univ Theatre Collection*

30759 Leyton Local Board of Health 4pp *Waltham Forest Archives*

30760 Stepney board of guardians 10pp *Greater London RO*

30761 London: St George in the East board of guardians 14pp *Greater London RO*

30762 Waltham Forest Archives: misc accessions 1p *Waltham Forest Archives*

30763 John Sampson, Romani scholar: corresp and papers 8pp *Liverpool Univ L*

30764 Charles Booth, shipowner and author: papers 11pp *Liverpool Univ L*

30765 Joseph Mayer, antiquary: corresp rel to Sprott's Chronicle 2pp *Liverpool Univ L*

30766 National and Local Government Officers Association: Abertillery and Tredegar branches 1p *Gwent RO*

30767 North Monmouthshire Hospital Management Committee 1p *Gwent RO*

30768 Birkenhead: Shaftesbury Boys Club 4pp *Wirral Archives*

30769 Alexander Hannay, proprietor of Grand Theatre, Glasgow: legal and financial papers 4pp *Glasgow Univ Archives*

30770 Robert Rendall, writer and poet: corresp and papers 23pp *Orkney AO*

30771 G & D Maxwell, potato merchants, Forfar 8pp *Dundee Univ L*

30772 Kirkwall Incorporation of Trades 14pp *Orkney AO*

30773 Glasgow Galloway Brotherly Society 4pp *Strathclyde Regional Archives*

30774 Pontypool: Jones' West Monmouthshire Grammar School 2pp *Gwent RO*

30775 Rhymney: Ramsden Street Methodist Church 2pp *Gwent RO*

30776 Abertillery: Ebenezer Baptist Church 2pp *Gwent RO*

30777 Ebbw Vale: Tabernacle Congregational Church 5pp *Gwent RO*

30778 Monmouthshire English Baptist Association and Monmouthshire Baptist Lay Preachers Union: Pontypool district 6pp *Gwent RO*

30779 Monmouthshire Baptist churches 11pp *Gwent RO*

30780 Glasgow University Graduates '93 Club 4pp *Glasgow Univ Archives*

30781 Glasgow Stevedores Association 3pp *Strathclyde Regional Archives*

30782 Charles Mann Fleming, professor of administrative medicine: corresp and papers 9pp *Glasgow Univ Archives*

30783 Macfie family of Langhouse and Beach: family and business papers 59pp *Glasgow Univ Archives*

30784 Rochford Hundred Amenities Society: MS collections 25pp *Essex RO, Southend*

30785 Shoeburyness and Thorpe Bay Baptist Church 18pp *Essex RO, Southend*

30786 Birkenhead and Wallasey Society of Friends 4pp *Wirral Archives*

30787 South-East Essex Baptist Fellowship 6pp *Essex RO, Southend*

30788 Leigh-on-Sea: Christ Church Free Church 1p *Essex RO, Southend*

30789 Essex schools 4pp *Essex RO and Essex RO, Southend*

30790 Morys Bruce, 4th Baron Aberdare: corresp and papers rel to history of tennis and rackets 2pp *Liverpool Univ Archives*

30791 Sir William Reynell Anson MP, warden of All Souls College, Oxford: corresp 13pp *All Souls Coll, Oxford*

30792 Oxford University: All Souls College estate papers 15pp *All Souls Coll, Oxford*

30793 Spirella Co of Great Britain Ltd, corset mfrs, Letchworth 2pp *First Garden City Heritage Mus*

30794 Alfred H Howe & Son, lace curtain mfrs, Nottingham 3pp *Notts RO*

30795 Electrical Association for Women: Bristol, Thornbury and Weston-super-Mare branches 1p *Bristol RO*

30796 George H Wheatcroft & Co Ltd, tape mfrs, Wirksworth 4pp *Derbys RO*

30797 F Braby & Co Ltd, engineers, Bristol and Deptford 2pp *Bristol RO*

30798 Bristol Law Students Society 6pp *Bristol RO*

30799 Bristol Chamber of Commerce and Industry 21pp *Bristol RO*

30800 Joseph Stone Hodges, furniture mfr and upholsterer, Bristol 3pp *Bristol RO*

30801 Bright family of Bristol: records relating to Bristol harbour 35pp *Bristol RO*

30802 Courage (Western) Ltd, brewers, Bristol: records of constituent companies 18pp *Bristol RO*

30803 Weston-super-Mare Methodist Circuit 3pp *Bristol RO*

30804 Mercers Company: Buckinghamshire and Bedfordshire manorial records (Colet and Chalgrave estates) 51pp *Private*

30805 National Dairy Council 9pp *History of Advertising Trust*

30806 Francis & John Lea, carpet mfrs, Kidderminster 1p *Kidderminster L, Heref and Worc*

30807 GP & J Baker Ltd, textile furnishings mfrs, London 8pp *Private*

30808 Bewdley Gas Light & Coke Co 5pp *Bewdley Mus, Heref and Worc*

30809 British and Foreign School Society 21pp *British and Foreign School Soc*

30810 Carrington Viyella Ltd, textile mfrs, Atherton 16pp *Lancs RO*

30811 Crompton family of High Crompton: papers incl records of A & A Crompton & Co Ltd, cotton spinners 5pp *Lancs RO*

30812 Ashworth family of Birtenshaw: corresp and papers 8pp *Lancs RO*

30813 C Whittaker & Co Ltd, engineers, Accrington 7pp *Accrington Central L, Lancs*

30814 JW Pickering & Sons Ltd, ship repairers, Liverpool 3pp *National Mus on Merseyside*

30815 Stitt family of Liverpool: business and family papers 4pp *National Mus on Merseyside*

30816 CBS Engineering Co, ship repairers, Liverpool 8pp *National Mus on Merseyside*

30817 Auckland Rural District Council 1p *Durham RO*

30818 East Durham Co-operative Chemists 1p *Durham RO*

30819 Tantobie Co-operative Society 1p *Durham RO*

30820 Washington Co-operative Society 1p *Durham RO*

30821 Towneley Co-operative Society: Stanley district 2pp *Durham RO*

30822 Durham City petty sessions 8pp *Durham RO*

30823 Bishop Auckland: Trinity United Reformed Church 5pp *Durham RO*

30824 Wandsworth and Fulham Methodist Circuit 3pp *Greater London RO*

30825 Staines and Feltham Methodist Circuit 7pp *Greater London RO*

30826 Aldam, Pease & Co, woollen merchants, Leeds 5pp *Doncaster Archives Dept*

30827 Exchequer Kings Remembrancer: exhibits 2pp *PRO, Chancery Lane*

30828 State Papers Supplementary: private papers 600pp *PRO, Chancery Lane*

30829 Rossendale Museum: business records 22pp *Rossendale Mus, Lancs*

30830 George Hardy, builders, Swanage 6pp *Dorset RO*

30831 Dorchester Rural District Council 25pp *Dorset RO*

30832 Malcolm John MacDonald, politician and diplomat: corresp and papers 169pp *Durham Univ Dept of Palaeography and Diplomatic*

30833 Boscombe United Reformed Church 10pp *Dorset RO*

30834 TG Burrell Ltd, department store, Chester 4pp *Chester City RO*

30835 Laurence Meakin Farrall, rector of Holy Trinity, Chester: corresp and papers 7pp *Chester City RO*

30836 Brintons Ltd, carpet mfrs, Kidderminster 11pp *Private*

30837 John Lowe & Bros, rope mfrs, Wribbenhall 5pp *Bewdley Mus, Heref and Worc*

30838 Hippisley family of Ston Easton: family and estate papers 87pp *Somerset RO*

30839 Yeatman-Biggs family of Stockton, Wilts: Somerset deeds and estate papers 23pp *Somerset RO*

30840 Earsham petty sessions 5pp *Norfolk RO*

30841 Thetford petty sessions 4pp *Norfolk RO*

30842 Norwich Primitive Methodist Circuit 1p *Norfolk RO*

30843 Hingham rural deanery 1p *Norfolk RO*

30844 Humbleyard rural deanery 1p *Norfolk RO*

30845 Anglian Water Authority 4pp *Norfolk RO*

30846 Norwich: Benevolent Association for the Relief of Decayed Tradesmen, Widows and Orphans 2pp *Norfolk RO*

30847 Norwich Charity Sports Committee 1p *Norfolk RO*

30848 Electrical Association for Women: Great Yarmouth and King's Lynn branches 1p *Norfolk RO*

30849 Norgate family: deeds, corresp and papers 4pp *Norfolk RO*

30850 Carleton family of Norwich: family and estate papers 5pp *Norfolk RO*

30851 Robert Pringle, pewterer, Spitalfields 1p *Hackney Archives Dept*

30852 Marla Ltd, ladies outfitters, Hackney 1p *Hackney Archives Dept*

30853 JR Spratling, writer and antiquary: papers 6pp *Hackney Archives Dept*

30854 Vaux Group plc, brewers, Sunderland 6pp *Private*

30855 King & Barnes Ltd, brewers, Horsham 12pp *Private*

30856 G Ruddle & Co plc, brewers, Langham 9pp *Private*

30857 Charles Wells Ltd, brewers, Bedford 34pp *Private*

30858 R Greg & Co Ltd, yarn spinners, Stockport 21pp *Stockport Central L*

30859 Birkenhead Brewery Co Ltd 2pp *Wirral Archives and Private*

30860 John H Fleming & Co Ltd, tanners, Warrington 4pp *Warrington Public L*

30861 William Dampier Jeans, solicitor, Warrington 1p *Warrington Public L*

30862 Goodyear Tyre & Rubber Co (Great Britain) Ltd, Wolverhampton 11pp *Wolverhampton Central L*

30863 General Sir James Murray-Pulteney, 7th Bt: corresp 18pp *Pierpont Morgan L, New York, USA*

30864 Caernarvonshire registers of duties on land values 9pp *Gwynedd Archives Service, Caernarfon*

30865 WJ Jarvis, Caernarvon: papers rel to North Wales 78pp *Gwynedd Archives Service, Caernarfon*

30866 Allied Breweries Ltd 116pp *Private*

30867 Everards Brewery Ltd, Narborough 5pp *Private*

30868 Tollemache & Cobbold Breweries Ltd, Ipswich 61pp *Private*

30869 Waldorf Astor, 2nd Viscount Astor: corresp and papers 30pp *Devon RO, Plymouth*

30870 West Devon registers of duties on land values 3pp *Devon RO, Plymouth*

30871 Lawrence Spear & Sons, solicitors, Plymouth 12pp *Devon RO, Plymouth*

30872 Tomkinsons Carpets Ltd, carpet mfrs, Kidderminster 14pp *Private*

30873 North Norfolk District Council 1p *Norfolk RO*

30874 Great Yarmouth District Council 1p *Norfolk RO*

30875 Hunstanton Convalescent Home Trust 1p *Norfolk RO*

30876 Arthur Bensly Whittingham, architect: corresp and papers 34pp *Norfolk RO*

30877 David Swynford Foulkes-
Roberts, teacher and
administrator in Nigeria:
diaries 4pp *Clwyd RO, Ruthin*

30878 Marshfield Congregational
Church 1p *Glos RO*

30879 Royal Gloucestershire Hussars
17pp *Glos RO*

30880 Thornbury Historical Society
4pp *Glos RO*

30881 Gloucester District Manpower
Committee 10pp *Glos RO*

30882 Shakespeare Society of
Cheltenham 3pp *Glos RO*

30883 Leslie Ranson, registrar of
Blackburn diocese: papers 11pp
Manchester Central L

30884 Amalgamated Society of
Woodworkers: Manchester
district 1p *Manchester Central L*

30885 Amalgamated Society of
Painters and Decorators:
Manchester No 1 branch 4pp
Manchester Central L

30886 Manchester Sacred Song
Association 2pp *Manchester
Central L*

30887 Beatrix Potter, author: literary
MSS, corresp and papers[1] 40pp
Private

30888 Rawtenstall District Library:
MS collection 78pp *Rawtenstall
District L, Lancs*

30889 W & A Gilbey Ltd, distillers,
Keith, Banffshire 6pp *Private*

30890 Royal Philosophical Society of
Glasgow 12pp *Glasgow Univ
Archives*

30891 Sir Maurice Edward Denny,
2nd Bt: corresp 5pp *Glasgow
Univ Archives*

30892 Glasgow University Early
Twenties Club 4pp *Glasgow
Univ Archives*

30893 Terence Reginald Forbes
Nonweiler, professor of
engineering: corresp and papers
9pp *Glasgow Univ Archives*

30894 DRG Packaging Ltd, Glasgow
10pp *Glasgow Univ Archives*

30895 Scottish Economic Society 4pp
Glasgow Univ Archives

30896 Donald James Robertson,
economist: corresp and papers
4pp *Glasgow Univ Archives*

30897 Sir Alexander Kirkland
Cairncross, economist: corresp
and papers 4pp *Glasgow Univ
Archives*

30898 Grosvenor family, Dukes of
Westminster: Halkyn deeds
and estate papers[2] 227pp *Clwyd
RO, Hawarden*

30899 North Eastern Marine
Engineering Co Ltd, Wallsend
11pp *Tyne and Wear Archives
Dept*

30900 Dartmouth Baptist churches
6pp *Devon RO*

30901 Cammell Laird Shipbuilders
Ltd, Birkenhead 2pp
Williamson Art Gallery and Mus

30902 Ettingshall: George Street
Methodist Church 2pp
Wolverhampton Central L

30903 Durham Diocesan Family
Welfare Council 10pp
Durham RO

30904 Bowes and Romaldkirk
Charity 27pp *Durham RO*

30905 Elwyn Jones & Co, solicitors,
Bangor: clients papers 90pp
*Gwynedd Archives Service,
Caernarfon*

30906 Caradog Jones of Mynytho:
corresp and papers 130pp
*Gwynedd Archives Service,
Caernarfon*

30907 Southern National Omnibus
Co Ltd 3pp *Devon RO*

30908 Torquay Cemetery Co 4pp
Devon RO

30909 Electrical Association for
Women: Ilfracombe, Tavistock
and Torquay branches 1p
Devon RO

30910 Exeter Ladies Hockey Club 1p
Devon RO

30911 West of England Fire & Life
Insurance Co, Exeter 1p
Devon RO

30912 Robert Hobart Mayo,
aeronautical engineer: papers
14pp *Science Mus L*

30913 Kent County Cricket Club 6pp
Kent AO

30914 Church of England Mens
Society: Rochester diocese 4pp
Kent AO

30915 Maidstone: Elms School 3pp
Kent AO

30916 West Kent Federation of
Womens Institutes 8pp
Kent AO

30917 Tenterden Young Mens
Mutual Improvement Society
2pp *Kent AO*

[1] L Linder *The Beatrix Potter Papers at Hill Top*, 1987   [2] CJ Williams *A Handlist of the Grosvenor (Halkyn) MSS*, 1988

30918 National Council of Women: Tunbridge Wells branch 2pp *Kent AO*

30919 Kent County Local History Committee 2pp *Kent AO*

30920 JW Hughes & Co, solicitors, Conway 20pp *Gwynedd Archives Service, Caernarfon*

30921 Evan Jones & Son, ironmongers and motor engineers, Carnarvon 50pp *Gwynedd Archives Service, Caernarfon*

30922 Amalgamated Union of Engineering Workers: Coventry district 3pp *Coventry City RO*

30923 Llandudno Permanent Benefit Building Society 35pp *Gwynedd Archives Service, Caernarfon*

30924 Thomas Coram Foundation for Children 180pp *Greater London RO*

30925 Holyhead & North Wales Gas & Water Co Ltd 80pp *Gwynedd Archives Service, Caernarfon*

30926 Henry Hainge, tailor and draper, Portmadoc 21pp *Gwynedd Archives Service, Caernarfon*

★30927 Edgeworth family of Edgeworthstown: corresp and literary papers 45pp *Bodleian L, Oxford*

30928 London Magistrates Clerks Association 3pp *Greater London RO*

30929 Coventry Precision Ltd, engineers: shop stewards committee 4pp *Warwick University Modern Records Centre*

30930 Association of Patternmakers and Allied Craftsmen 8pp *Warwick University Modern Records Centre*

30931 Lichfield United Reformed Church 3pp *Lichfield Joint RO*

30932 Staffordshire registers of duties on land values 9pp *Staffs RO*

30933 National Union of Mineworkers: Midlands area 7pp Staffs RO

30934 Audley and Hardingswood Educational and Relief Charity 11pp *Staffs RO*

30935 Yoxall Town Land Trustees 8pp *Staffs RO*

30936 Cannock Conduit Trust 16pp *Staffs RO*

30937 Stafford: Church Lane Evangelical Church 1p *Staffs RO*

30938 Stoke-on-Trent: Shelton New Road Providence Chapel 1p *Staffs RO*

30939 Bickford family of Bickington: papers 6pp *Devon RO, Plymouth*

30940 Charity Commission: West Devon charities accounts 15pp *Devon RO, Plymouth*

30941 Shelton Iron, Steel & Coal Co Ltd, Etruria 3pp *Staffs RO*

30942 JD Bebbington, estate agent, Endon 28pp *Staffs RO*

30943 Hodgson family of Uttoxeter: deeds and estate papers 4pp *Staffs RO*

30944 Bradley School Endowed Trust 5pp *Staffs RO*

30945 Ward family of Leek: family and estate papers 8pp *Staffs RO*

30946 Amalgamated Association of Operative Cotton Spinners and Twiners 2pp *Preston District L*

30947 Tower Hamlets Local History Library: misc accessions 4pp *Tower Hamlets Local History L*

30948 Fox Brothers & Co Ltd, woollen mfrs, Wellington 28pp *Private*

30949 Thomas Hughes, antiquary and bookseller: corresp, papers and Cheshire collection 80pp *Chester City RO*

30950 Wendy Wood, Scottish nationalist: corresp and papers 5pp *National L of Scotland*

30951 Duncan Fraser, publisher and author: corresp and papers 9pp *National L of Scotland*

30952 Kathleen Goldie, author: corresp and papers 23pp *National L of Scotland*

30953 Isobel Wylie Hutchison, author: corresp and papers 2pp *National L of Scotland*

30954 James Johnstone, MP: diaries 1p *National L of Scotland*

30955 The Jewish Museum: MS collection 51pp *Jewish Mus, London*

30956 Epsom Baptist Church 1p *Surrey RO, Kingston*

30957 Courtaulds plc, textile mfrs, London: design archive 17pp *Private*

30958 K Shoemakers Ltd, Kendal 6pp *Private*

30959 Bethnal Green Road Congregational Church 2pp *Tower Hamlets Local History L*

30960 Cambridge University Common Court 118pp *Cambridge Univ Archives*

30961 Thomas Pratt & Sons Ltd, clerical tailors 2pp *Westminster Archives Dept*

30962 Sir David Young Cameron and Katharine Cameron, painters and etchers: corresp and papers 4pp *National L of Scotland*

30963 Thomas Carlyle, essayist and historian: family corresp and papers 27pp *National L of Scotland*

30964 Mackintosh family of Geddes, Nairn: estate papers 4pp *Private*

30965 Equitable Loan Company of Scotland Ltd 3pp *Private*

30966 Wood, Brown and Graham families of Edinburgh: business and family corresp and papers 27pp *Various locations*

30967 Marshall, Fleming & Co Ltd, engineers and crane builders, Motherwell 10pp *Glasgow Univ Archives*

30968 The Bridge of Weir Leather Co Ltd 8pp *Private*

30969 Liberal Party: South Edinburgh association 1p *National L of Scotland*

30970 Dundee United Evangelistic Association and Tent Mission 10pp *Dundee Archive Centre*

30971 Dundee Educational Trust 3pp *Dundee Archive Centre*

30972 William Goodacre & Sons Ltd, carpet and cocoanut matting mfrs, Holme 2pp *Cumbria RO, Kendal*

30973 Braithwaite & Co Ltd, woollen mfrs, Kendal 9pp *Cumbria RO, Kendal*

30974 Isaac Braithwaite & Son, engineers and drysalters, Kendal 10pp *Cumbria RO, Kendal*

30975 Robert R Buck & Sons Ltd, woollen mfrs, Carlisle 11pp *Cumbria RO, Carlisle*

30976 Thorpe & Co Ltd, tailors and warehousemen, Carlisle 5pp *Cumbria RO, Carlisle*

30977 St Martin's Langdale Linen Industry 3pp *Cumbria RO, Kendal*

30978 Crewdson family of Helme Lodge, Westmorland: business and family papers 7pp *Cumbria RO, Kendal*

30979 Arnold, Greenwood & Son, solicitors, Kendal 3pp *Cumbria RO, Kendal*

30980 Milne, Moser & Sons, solicitors, Kendal 1p *Cumbria RO, Kendal*

30981 CG Thomson & Wilson, solicitors, Kendal 1p *Cumbria RO, Kendal*

30982 Stead McAlpin & Co Ltd, calico printers, Cummersdale 1p *Cumbria RO, Carlisle*

30983 Cumbria Record Office, Kendal: misc accessions 1p *Cumbria RO, Kendal*

30984 Franz Hildebrandt, theologian: corresp and papers 8pp *National L of Scotland*

30985 Bowes Manor: deeds, manorial and estate papers 42pp *Durham RO*

30986 Barrow Hepburn Group plc 12pp *Private*

30987 Electrical Association for Women: Cheshire branches 1p *Cheshire RO*

30988 Eckersleys Ltd, cotton spinners, Wigan 3pp *Wigan RO*

30989 Pennington Mill Co Ltd, cotton goods mfrs, Leigh 6pp *Wigan RO*

30990 Fine Cotton Spinners and Doublers Association Ltd 1p *Wigan RO*

30991 MacDonnell family of Belfast, Dublin and Kilsharvan, Co Meath: corresp and family papers 25pp *PRO of N Ireland*

30992 Shepherd & Woodward, tailors, Oxford 1p *Oxon RO*

30993 Marshall & Co, flax spinners, Leeds 8pp *Brotherton L, Leeds Univ*

30994 Thomas Jones, economist and public servant: corresp and papers 700pp *National L of Wales*

30995 Ovenden: Providence United Reformed Church 8pp *Calderdale District Archives*

30996 William Rought Ltd, hatters' furriers, Brandon 13pp *Suffolk RO, Bury St Edmunds*

30997 Bury St Edmunds Clerical Society 1p *Suffolk RO, Bury St Edmunds*

30998 Ipswich Methodist Circuit 5pp *Suffolk RO, Ipswich and Suffolk RO, Bury St Edmunds*

30999 Scottish Convention of Women 8pp *National L of Scotland*

31000 Burnley Co-operative Society Ltd 3pp *Burnley Central L, Lancs*

31001 Burnley: Trafalgar Street Unitarian Church 1p *Burnley Central L, Lancs*

31002 John Fletcher and Sons, cotton spinners, Ashton-under-Lyne 5pp *Tameside Local Studies L*

31003 Hugh Kershaw & Sons Ltd, woollen mfrs, Mossley 23pp *Tameside Local Studies L*

31004 Victor Mill Ltd, cotton mfrs, Stalybridge 10pp *Tameside Local Studies L*

31005 Staley & Millbrook Ltd, cotton spinners, Stalybridge 8pp *Tameside Local Studies L*

31006 Cedar Mill, cotton spinners, Ashton-under-Lyne 5pp *Tameside Local Studies L*

31007 Newton Mill Ltd, stationery mfrs, Hyde 2pp *Tameside L, Hyde*

31008 Kelso Races Ltd 1p *National L of Scotland*

31009 Labour Party: South Leeds constituency 7pp *Leeds District Archives*

31010 Pudsey Civic Society 2pp *Leeds District Archives*

31011 Leeds Discharged Prisoners Aid Society 1p *Leeds District Archives*

31012 Robinson & Birdsell Ltd, scrap merchants, Leeds 2pp *Leeds District Archives*

31013 Yorkshire Ramblers Club 1p *Leeds District Archives*

31014 Oliver, Kitchen & Flynn, estate agents, auctioneers and valuers, Leeds 2pp *Leeds District Archives*

31015 Electrical Association for Women: Wetherby and district branch 1p *Leeds District Archives*

31016 Joshua Todd & Son, ironfounders, Summerbridge 1p *Leeds District Archives*

31017 William Douglas-Home, playwright: corresp and papers 22pp *National L of Scotland*

31018 National League of the Blind and Disabled: Scottish district council 1p *National L of Scotland*

31019 Preston District Library: misc accessions 4pp *Preston District L*

31020 Bury Art Gallery and Museum: MS collection 33pp *Bury Art Gallery and Mus*

31021 Creskeld estate plans 3pp *Private*

31022 Wright & Appleton, solicitors, Wigan 100pp *Wigan RO*

31023 Liberal Party: Kinross-shire association 1p *National L of Scotland*

31024 John Bright & Brothers Ltd, cotton spinners and mfrs, Rochdale 2pp *Rochdale Central L*

31025 Ingham Womersley Ltd, woollen and worsted serge mfrs, Pudsey 7pp *Leeds District Archives*

31026 Kitchin & Co Ltd, tanners, Leeds 1p *Leeds District Archives*

31027 James Armitage & Sons, cloth finishers, Leeds 1p *Leeds District Archives*

31028 Ford Ayrton & Co Ltd silk spinners, Bentham 28pp *Leeds District Archives*

31029 Thomas Wright & Co Ltd, leather dressers, Leeds 5pp *Leeds District Archives*

31030 Totty & Son, hosiers and outfitters, Leeds 1p *Leeds District Archives*

31031 William Paul Ltd, tanners, Leeds 1p *Leeds District Archives*

31032 John Wilson (Gildersome) Ltd, woollen mfrs, Gildersome and Morley 1p *Leeds District Archives*

31033 Baker family of Leytonstone: family and estate papers 7pp *Waltham Forest Archives*

31034 Woodward Grosvenor & Co Ltd, carpet mfrs, Kidderminster 10pp *Private*

31035 Small & Co, ship and insurance brokers and Lloyds agents, Lowestoft 1p *Suffolk RO, Lowestoft*

31036 Colby Fish Selling Co Ltd, Lowestoft 25pp *Suffolk RO, Lowestoft*

31037 Lowestoft Harbour 1p *Suffolk RO, Lowestoft*

31038 Sir George Taylor, botanist: corresp and papers 9pp *National L of Scotland*

31039 Bungay: Outney Common Owners 7pp *Suffolk RO, Lowestoft*

31040 Oulton Poor Land Trustees 1p *Suffolk RO, Lowestoft*

31041 Dodds & Co, drapers, Alnwick 4pp *Northumberland RO*

31042 George Matthewson & Sons, drapers, grocers and hatters, Branxton 2pp *Northumberland RO*

31043 Northill Methodist Circuit 10pp *Cornwall RO*

31044 Edyvean family of Bodmin: family and estate papers 2pp *Cornwall RO*

31045 Cornwall Productivity Association 5pp *Cornwall RO*

31046 Cornwall rural deaneries 26pp *Cornwall RO*

31047 Truro diocese 15pp *Cornwall RO*

31048 Archdeaconry of Cornwall 6pp *Cornwall RO*

31049 South West Water Authority 32pp *Cornwall RO*

31050 British Broadcasting Corporation 14pp *BBC Written Archives Centre*

31051 Ronald Middleton Farquhar, Church of Scotland minister: corresp and papers 21pp *National L of Scotland*

31052 Henry Charles Whitley, Church of Scotland minister: corresp and papers 7pp *National L of Scotland*

31053 Edinburgh Festival Society Ltd 1p *National L of Scotland*

31054 Norwest Pioneers Co-operative Society Ltd: records of predecessor societies 4pp *Rochdale Central L*

31055 Corah plc, underwear, outerwear and hosiery mfrs, Leicester 7pp *Private*

31056 Standard Mill (Rochdale) Ltd, cotton spinners and doublers 4pp *Rochdale Central L*

31057 John Ormerod & Sons Ltd, leather dressers and finishers, Rochdale 3pp *Rochdale Central L*

31058 Samuel Heap & Sons Ltd, bleachers, dyers and finishers, Rochdale 1p *Rochdale Central L*

31059 Glamorganshire Banking Co, Neath 7pp *Lloyds Bank Archives*

31060 Rochdale Canal Co 4pp *Rochdale Central L*

31061 Rochdale Central Library: misc accessions 6pp *Rochdale Central L*

31062 Bent Ley Silk Mills Ltd, Meltham 1p *Kirklees District Archives*

31063 Wilton Royal Carpet Factory Ltd 10pp *Private*

31064 William Fison & Co, worsted spinners, Burley in Wharfedale 29pp *Bradford District Archives*

31065 John Broadbent & Son Ltd, woollen mfrs and merchants, Longwood 12pp *Kirklees District Archives*

31066 Chrispin of Huddersfield Ltd, woollen mfrs 6pp *Kirklees District Archives*

31067 W & E Crowther Ltd, woollen mfrs, Slaithwaite 2pp *Kirklees District Archives*

31068 Jonathan Gomersal, worsted spinners, Gomersal 2pp *Kirklees District Archives*

31069 John Lockwood & Sons Ltd, woollen mfrs, Milnsbridge 4pp *Kirklees District Archives*

31070 GH Norton & Co Ltd, fancy cloth mfrs, Scissett 10pp *Kirklees District Archives*

31071 James Sykes Ltd, worsted mfrs, Milnsbridge 1p *Kirkless District Archives*

31072 JE Taylor Bros, woollen mfrs, Almondbury 1p *Kirklees District Archives*

31073 B Vickerman & Sons Ltd, worsted mfrs, Holmbridge 3pp *Kirklees District Archives*

31074 Hereford & Tredegar Brewery Ltd 10pp *Heref and Worc RO, Hereford*

31075 Toc H: Leominster branch 2pp *Heref and Worc RO, Hereford*

31076 Hereford Methodist Circuit 4pp *Heref and Worc RO, Hereford*

31077 London & North Eastern Railway Co 35pp *Durham RO*

31078 Herefordshire registers of duties on land values 6pp *Heref and Worc RO, Hereford*

31079 Essex Family Practitioner Committee 11pp *Essex RO*

31080 Hirsch Son & Rhodes Ltd, top mfrs, Bradford 20pp *Bradford District Archives*

31081 Essex Home School 19pp *Essex RO*

31082 Era Ring Mill Ltd, cotton spinners, Rochdale 8pp *Rochdale Central L*

31083 Charity Commission: Herefordshire charities accounts 3pp *Heref and Worc RO, Hereford*

31084 Ross Endowed Charities 4pp *Heref and Worc RO, Hereford*

31085 Barbara Leigh Smith Bodichon, painter and campaigner for women's rights: corresp and papers 11pp *Girton Coll, Cambridge*

31086 Callander family of Prestonhall: family and estate papers 94pp *Private*

31087 Morrison's Bowmore Distillery Ltd, whisky distillers, Glasgow 8pp *Private*

31088 Scobie & McIntosh Ltd, bakery and catering equipment mfrs, Edinburgh 5pp *Private*

31089 Andrew Mitchell & Co Ltd, canvas mfrs, Glasgow 4pp *Glasgow Univ Archives*

31090 Andrew Usher & Co, distillers and wine and spirit merchants, Edinburgh 4pp *Private*

31091 Malcolm McNeill Ltd, haulage contractors, Glasgow 5pp *Private*

31092 R & W Scott Ltd, marmalade and preserve mfrs, Carluke, Lanarkshire 7pp *Private*

31093 Salisbury United Reformed Church 6pp *Wilts RO*

31094 Samuel Moore & Sons Ltd, fruit preserves mfrs, Easterton 2pp *Wilts RO*

31095 Trowbridge Chamber of Commerce 2pp *Wilts RO*

31096 Chapmanslade United Reformed Church 2pp *Wilts RO*

31097 Westbury Chamber of Commerce 1p *Wilts RO*

31098 Shrewton Flood Charity 2pp *Wilts RO*

31099 Jean Frederick Ostervald, protestant theologian: corresp 4pp *Neuchatel Archives, Switzerland*

31100 National Savings Movement: Essex committees 7pp *Essex RO*

31101 Eastwood: Bridgewater Drive United Reformed Church 3pp *Essex RO, Southend*

31102 Reading Dispensary Trust 7pp *Berks RO*

31103 Wantage Rural Deanery 2pp *Berks RO*

31104 Newbury rural deanery 3pp *Berks RO*

31105 Provident Mutual Life Assurance Association 23pp *Guildhall L, London*

31106 Loughton Brotherhood 3pp *Essex RO*

31107 Victoria County History of Essex 14pp *Essex RO*

31108 Newbury: Weavers Company 4pp *Berks RO*

31109 A & S Henry & Co (Dundee) Ltd, textile mfrs and merchants 77pp *Dundee Univ L*

31110 Griffith Jones, solicitor, Caernarvon, 130pp *Gwynedd Archives Service, Caernarfon*

31111 Ellis Davies & Co, solicitors, Caernarvon 34pp *Gwynedd Archives Service, Caernarfon*

31112 Lloyds Bank Ltd, Caernarvon branch 11pp *Lloyds Bank Archives*

31113 Monmouthshire and South Wales Coalowners Association 122pp *National L of Wales*

31114 Cowell-Stepney family, baronets, of Prendergast and Llanelli: family and estate papers 69pp *National L of Wales*

31115 Stead, McAlpin & Co Ltd, calico printers, Cummersdale 24pp *Private*

31116 Carpenter-Holland-Griffith family of Carreglwyd: family and estate papers 480pp *National L of Wales*

31117 Vaughan family of Courtfield: estate papers 94pp *National L of Wales*

31118 Loughrea Priory 4pp *Private*

31119 Bon Marché Ltd, department store, Brixton 12pp *Private*

31120 Heelas Ltd, drapers, Reading 8pp *Private*

31121 George Smith & Sons Ltd, furriers, London 7pp *Westminster Archives Dept*

31122 Reeves family of Besborough: estate corresp 13pp *Private*

31123 Domvile family, baronets, of Templeogue: family and estate papers 8pp *National L of Ireland*

31124 Scottish College of Textiles: business records collection 30pp *Scottish Coll of Textiles*

31125 Museum of Leathercraft: MS collections 15pp *Mus of Leathercraft, Northampton*

★31126 Society for the Protection of Science and Learning 210pp *Bodleian L, Oxford*

31127 Priday, Metford & Co Ltd, flour millers, Gloucester 14pp *Glos RO*

31128 WJB Halls Ltd, builders and joiners, Gloucester 1p *Glos RO*

31129 John Williams & Co, coal merchants, Cheltenham 3pp *Glos RO*

31130 Blakeney Congregational Church 2pp *Glos RO*

31131 Avening Baptist Church 2pp *Glos RO*

31132 Toc H: Gloucestershire branches 4pp *Glos RO*

31133 Helipebs Ltd, grinding machinery mfrs, Gloucester 3pp *Glos RO*

★31134 Kenneth Bailey, biochemist: corresp and papers 14pp *Cambridge Univ L*

*31135   Arthur Roderick Collar, aeronautical engineer: corresp and papers 22pp *Bristol Univ L*

*31136   Sir Harold Warris Thompson, chemist: corresp and papers 212pp *Royal Soc*

31137   Smith-Barry family of Marbury Hall, Cheshire and Fota Island: deeds and estate papers 5pp *Private*

31138   Perry family of Cork: deeds and papers 17pp *Private*

31139   De la Poer family, Counts de la Poer: family and estate papers 24pp *Private*

31140   Maxwell family, Barons Farnham: family and estate papers 2pp *National L of Ireland*

31141   Eustace-Duckett family of Castlemore: family and estate papers 2pp *Private*

31142   Proby family, Earls of Carysfort: deeds and estate papers 16pp *National L of Ireland*

31143   H Kieran of Ardee: papers rel to Verdon family 76pp *Private*

31144   Walsh family of Castlebellingham: family and estate papers 4pp *Private*

31145   Barton family of Grove: family and estate papers 18pp *Private*

31146   Baker family of Ballytobin: family and estate papers 43pp *National L of Ireland and Private*

31147   Chetwode family of Woodbrook: family and estate papers 4pp *Private*

31148   Acton family of Stradbrook House, co Dublin and West Aston, co Wicklow: family and estate papers 14pp *Private*

31149   National Library of Ireland: misc accessions 41pp *National L of Ireland*

31150   Dillon family, Barons Clonbrock: family and estate papers 56pp *National L of Ireland*

31151   Doyne family of Wells: family and estate papers 4pp *Private*

31152   Kavanagh family of Borris: family and estate papers 21pp *Private*

31153   Loftus family of Mount Loftus: family and estate papers 15pp *Private*

31154   Madden family of Hilton: family and estate papers 27pp *PRO of N Ireland and Private*

31155   Mahon family of Strokestown: family and estate papers 61pp *Private*

31156   Mansfield family of Morristown Lattin: family and estate papers 44pp *National L of Ireland*

31157   Ram family of Clonattin: family and estate papers 6pp *National L of Ireland*

31158   Ridgeway family of Ballydermott: deeds and papers 14pp *National L of Ireland*

31159   National Library of Ireland: reports on collections in private possession 136pp *Private*

31160   Bruen family of Oak Park: family and estate papers 15pp *National L of Ireland and Private*

31161   Coddington family of Oldbridge: family and estate papers 8pp *Private*

31162   St Leger family, Viscounts Doneraile: family and estate papers 51p *National L of Ireland*

31163   Filgate family of Lissrenny: family and estate papers 4pp *National L of Ireland and Private*

31164   Fitzsimon family of Annaghmakerrig: family and estate papers 12pp *Private*

31165   Grove Annesley family of Annesgrove: family and estate papers 6pp *Private*

31166   Hamilton-Russell family, Viscounts Boyne: Stackallen deeds and papers 11pp *Private*

31167   Wingfield family, Viscounts Powerscourt: family and estate papers 13pp *National L of Ireland and Private*

31168   Johnson–Walsh family, baronets, of Ballykilcavan: family and estate papers 13pp *Private*

31169   Wolfe family of Forenaghts: family and estate papers 10pp *National L of Ireland*

31170   Aylward family of Shankill: family and estate papers 6pp *Private*

31171   Browne–Clayton family of Browne's Hill: family and estate papers 5pp *Private*

31172   Herbert family of Muckruss: family and estate papers 9pp *PRO of Ireland*

31173   London Transport 4pp *Greater London RO*

31174   Lombard family of Lombardstown: family and estate papers 72pp *National L of Ireland*

31175 Guido Gezelle, chaplain of the English Convent at Bruges: corresp and papers 16pp *Bruges City L*

31176 Mahon family, baronets, of Castlegar: family and estate papers 22pp *National L of Ireland*

31177 Riall family of Old Conna Hill: family and estate papers 12pp *National L of Ireland and Private*

31178 Joseph Bridge, organist and composer: corresp and papers rel to Chester Music Festival 9pp *Chester City RO*

31179 Smyth family of Drumcree: family and estate papers 30pp *Private*

31180 Sweetman family of Drumbaragh: family and estate papers 10pp *Private*

31181 Tottenham family of Ballycurry: family and estate papers 10pp *Private*

31182 White family of Peppards Castle: family and estate papers 7pp *National L of Ireland and Private*

31183 Kemeys-Tynte, family of Halswell, Somerset, and Cefn Mably, Glam: family and estate papers 70pp *Somerset RO*

31184 Bayly family of Ballyarthur: family and estate papers 28pp *Private*

31185 McClintock-Bunbury family, Barons Rathdonnell: Lisnavagh estate papers 2pp *Private*

31186 Donovan family of Ballymore: family and estate papers 24pp *Private*

31187 Thomas Robinson, 2nd Baron Grantham and Frederick Robinson MP: family corresp 28pp *Devon RO, Plymouth*

31188 Verschoyle family of Kilberry: Mounttown deeds and papers 7pp *Private*

31189 Dunne family of Brittas: family and estate papers 27pp *Private*

31190 Hely-Hutchinson family of Seafield: family and estate papers 4pp *Private*

31191 Stafford-King-Harman family, baronets, of Rockingham: family and estate papers 4pp *Private*

31192 Naper family of Loughcrew: family and estate papers 20pp *Private*

31193 Sir George Treby, judge: corresp 5pp *Derbys RO*

31194 O'Byrne family of Allardstown: family and estate papers 11pp *National L of Ireland*

31195 O'Callaghan-Westropp family of Maryfort: family and estate papers 25pp *National L of Ireland*

31196 Dawson-Damer family, Earls of Portarlington: family and estate papers 3pp *National L of Ireland*

31197 Royal Naval Constructive Officers Mutual and Death Benefit Association: Chatham, Devonport and Portsmouth branches 2pp *Devon RO, Plymouth*

31198 Boyd-Rochfort family of Middleton: family and estate papers 2pp *Private*

31199 Atkinson family of Cangort: family and estate papers 9pp *Private*

31200 Bellew family, Barons Bellew: family and estate papers 4pp *Private*

31201 Blood family of Ballykilty: family and estate papers 3pp *Private*

31202 Boxwell family of Butlerstown: family and estate papers 19pp *Private*

31203 Colclough family of Tintern Abbey: family and estate papers 16pp *National L of Ireland*

31204 Cooper family of Killenure: family and estate papers 4pp *Private*

31205 Wentworth-Fitzwilliam family, Earls Fitzwilliam: Irish estate papers 3pp *National L of Ireland*

31206 Grattan-Bellew family, baronets, of Mount Bellew: family and estate papers 5pp *National L of Ireland*

31207 Medlicott family of Dunmurry: family and estate papers 4pp *National L of Ireland and Private*

31208 Montgomery family of Beaulieu: family and estate papers 12pp *Private*

31209 Nesbitt family of Tubberdaly: family and estate papers 8pp *Private*

31210 Newenham family of Coolmore: estate papers 2pp *National L of Ireland*

31211 Nugent family, baronets, of Cloncoskoraine: family and estate papers 6pp *Private*

31212 O'Brien family of Ballyalla: family and estate papers 16pp *National L of Ireland*

31213 O'Malley family of Suir Castle: family and estate papers 18pp *Private*

31214 Reynell family of Killynon: family and estate papers 5pp *Private*

31215 St Lawrence family, Earls Howth: deeds and papers 6pp *Private*

31216 Shaw family, baronets, of Bushy Park: family and estate papers 11pp *Private*

31217 Somerville family of Drishane: family and estate papers 4pp *Private*

31218 Taaffe family of Smarmore: family and estate papers 3pp *Private*

31219 Prior-Wandesforde family of Castlecomer: family and estate papers 7pp *Various locations*

31220 White family, Earls of Bantry: family and estate papers 20pp *Private*

31221 Anderson family of Grace Dieu: family and estate papers 3pp *Private*

31222 Biddulph family of Rathrobin and Fortal: family and estate papers 3pp *Private*

31223 Bomford family of Oakley Park: family and estate papers 4pp *Private*

31224 Congreve family of Mount Congreve: family and estate papers 11pp *Private*

31225 O'Donovan family of Clan Cathal: family and estate papers 33pp *Private*

31226 Hickie family of Kilelton: family and estate papers 4pp *Private*

31227 Keane family, baronets, of Cappoquin: family and estate papers 4pp *Private*

31228 Nevill family of Forenaghts: deeds and estate papers 5pp *Private*

31229 Paul family, baronets, of Ballyglan: family and estate papers 5pp *National L of Ireland*

31230 Penrose family of Riverview: family and estate papers 6pp *Trinity Coll L, Dublin*

31231 Orpen family of Ardtully: family and estate papers 11pp *Private*

31232 Plunkett family of Portmarnock: family and estate papers 15pp *National L of Ireland*

31233 Truell family of Clonmannon: family and estate papers 10pp *Private*

31234 Vigors family of Burgage: family and estate papers 12pp *PRO of Ireland*

31235 Plunkett family, Barons Louth: family and estate papers 87pp *Private*

31236 Nugent family of Farren Connell: family and estate papers 89pp *Private*

31237 O'Shee family of Gardenmorris: family and estate papers 59pp *National L of Ireland*

31238 Colonel Philip Doyne Vigors: MS collection 44pp *Private*

31239 Leslie-Ellis family of Magherymore: family and estate papers 4pp *Private*

31240 Everard family of Randlestown: family and estate papers 19pp *Private*

31241 Gabbett family of Caherline: family and estate papers 6pp *Private*

31242 La Touche family of Bellevue: corresp and papers 5pp *Private*

*31243 Upcher family of Sheringham: family and estate papers 63pp *Norfolk RO*

31244 Palmer family, baronets, of Castle Lacken: family and estate papers 13pp *Private*

31245 Vance & Co, solicitors, Bailieborough: clients papers 40pp *National L of Ireland*

31246 John Wilson Patten, Baron Winmarleigh: corresp and family papers 37pp *Lancs RO*

31247 Fock family, Barons De Robeck: family and estate papers 3pp *Private*

31248 Browne family, Marquesses of Sligo: family and estate papers 3pp *Private*

31249 Prideaux-Brune family of Prideaux Place: family and estate papers 8pp *Cornwall RO*

31250 Royal Society of Antiquaries of Ireland: MS collections 11pp *Royal Soc of Antiquaries of Ireland, Dublin*

31251 Dublin: Apothecaries Hall 4pp *Private*

31252 Athy Borough 3pp *Private*

31253 Carlow: St Patrick's College 1p *Private*

31254 Clibborn family of Moate: family and estate papers 4pp *Private*

31255 Ennis family of Newbawn: family and estate papers 2pp *Private*

31256 Finlay family of Corkagh: family and estate papers 5pp *Private*

31257 Waterford: Bishop Foy School 1p *Private*

31258 Dublin: Genealogical Office 3pp *Private*

31259 Ron Evans, Ebbw Vale Constituency Labour Party secretary: political corresp and papers 12pp *National L of Wales*

31260 Davis-Goff family, baronets, of Glenville and Horetown: family and estate papers 8pp *Private*

31261 Grand Canal Co, Dublin 1p *Private*

31262 Leslie family, baronets, of Glaslough: family and estate papers 4pp *National L of Ireland and Private*

31263 Meath Grand Juries 2pp *Private*

31264 New Ross Borough 2pp *Private*

31265 Daniell & Co, East India merchants, London 7pp *Guildhall L, London*

31266 Parkinson family of Red House, Ardee: family and estate papers 14pp *Private*

31267 Richards family of Solsborough: deeds and papers 4pp *Private*

31268 Society of Licensed Victuallers 8pp *Guildhall L, London*

31269 Trim Borough 11pp *Private*

31270 Waterford Dean and Chapter 3pp *Private*

31271 Wexford Borough 2pp *Private*

31272 Wicklow Borough 4pp *Private*

31273 Joseph Barber & Co Ltd, wharfingers and warehouse keepers, London 5pp *Guildhall L, London*

31274 Butler family of Castle Crine: deeds and papers 5pp *National L of Ireland*

31275 National Pawnbrokers Association 9pp *Guildhall L, London*

31276 Lucas-Clements family of Rathkenny: family and estate papers 2pp *Private*

31277 Grove family of Castle Grove: family and estate papers 5pp *Private*

31278 Farebrother, Ellis & Co, land and estate agents, surveyors and auctioneers, London 9pp *Guildhall L, London*

31279 Heseltine, Powell & Co, stockbrokers, London 7pp *Guildhall L London*

31280 Union Society of London 7pp *Guildhall L, London*

31281 Imperial Contintental Gas Associaton, London 33pp *Guildhall L, London*

31282 Antwerp Waterworks Co Ltd, London 3pp *Guildhall L, London*

31283 Ede & Ravenscroft Ltd, robemakers, tailors and wigmakers, London 16pp *Guildhall L, London*

31284 National Benevolent Society of Watch and Clock Makers 12pp *Guildhall L, London*

31285 Exchange Telegraph Co Ltd, London 44pp *Guildhall L, London*

31286 Holtzapffel & Co, mechanical engineers, lathe and tool makers, London 10pp *Guildhall L, London*

31287 Camp Bird Ltd, gold miners, London 22pp *Guildhall L, London*

31288 Morgan Grenfell & Co Ltd, merchant bankers, London 21pp *Guildhall L, London*

31289 Metropolitan Public Gardens Association 11pp *Guildhall L, London*

31290 Samuel Pepys, diarist: family corresp and papers 11pp *Guildhall L, London*

31291 Rivington & Son, solicitors, London 4pp *Guildhall L, London*

31292 Parker, Garrett & Co, solicitors, London 4pp *Guildhall L, London*

31293 Emery family of London and Ely: corresp and papers 3pp *Guildhall L, London*

31294 Robert Phillips Whellock, architect: sketchbooks and personal papers incl religious diary 3pp *Guildhall L, London*

31295 Phillips family of Gaile: family and estate papers 1p *Private*

31296 Roch family of Woodbine Hill: family and estate papers 3pp *Private*

31297 Tisdall family of Charlesfort: family and estate papers 28pp *Private*

31298 Waterford diocese 1p *Private*
31299 Dundee Young Mens Christian Association 5pp *Dundee Archive Centre*
31300 Aberdeen Medico-Chirurgical Society 34pp *Private*
31301 Dundee Highland Society 3pp *Dundee Archive Centre*
31302 Crofton family of Inchinappa: family and estate papers 2pp *National L of Ireland and Private*
31303 D'Arcy family of Hyde Park: family and estate papers 9pp *Private*
31304 Levinge family, baronets, of Knockdrin: family and estate papers 1p *National L of Ireland*
31305 Raimes, Clark & Co Ltd, wholesale chemists, Leith 9pp *Private*
31306 O'Donnell family, baronets, of Newport: family and estate papers 2pp *National L of Ireland*
31307 Rolleston family of Franckfort: family and estate papers 2pp *National L of Ireland and Private*
31308 Sarsfield family of Doughcloyne: family and estate papers 61pp *Private*
31309 Standish family of Rathbeggan: family and estate papers 1p *Private*
31310 Wilson-Slator family of White Hill: family and estate papers 3pp *National L of Ireland*
31311 Crofton family, Barons Crofton: family and estate papers 3pp *National L of Ireland*
31312 Dundee Parliament 3pp *Dundee Archive Centre*
31313 Simpson Label Co Ltd, Dalkeith 7pp *Private*
31314 Dundee Citizens Advice Bureau 3pp *Dundee Archive Centre*
31315 Carnoustie Young Mens Christian Association 3pp *Private*
31316 Arbroath Congregational Church 6pp *Dundee Archive Centre*
31317 Dundee, Perth and Blairgowrie Methodist Circuit 11pp *Dundee Archive Centre*
31318 D Pirie & Co (1931) Ltd, jute merchants, Dundee 3pp *Private*
31319 Bessie Rayner Parkes, author, journalist and campaigner for women's rights; corresp and papers 62pp *Girton Coll, Cambridge*

31320 Annesley family, Viscounts Valentia: Wexford deeds and papers 3pp *National L of Ireland*
31321 Blood family of Cranagher: family and estate papers 5pp *Private*
31322 Wogan-Browne family of Castle Browne: family and estate papers 9pp *Private*
31323 Blunden family, baronets, of Castle Blunden: family and estate papers 1p *Private*
31324 Coffey family of Glendarragh: family papers 1p *Private*
31325 De Butts family of Coolnakilly: family and estate papers 6pp *Private*
31326 Dopping-Hepenstal family of Derrycassan: family and estate papers 3pp *National L of Ireland*
31327 Captain Robert FitzGerald, Bombay Army: corresp and papers 5pp *India Office L*
31328 Lindesay family of Loughry: family and estate papers 1p *National L of Ireland*
31329 Minchin family of Busherstown: family and estate papers 2pp *National L of Ireland*
31330 John Russell Colvin and Sir Elliot Graham Colvin, Indian civil servants: diaries and papers 3pp *India Office L*
31331 Arthur Kingscote Potter, civil servant: corresp 2pp *India Office L*
31332 JR Stewart & Sons, solicitors, Dublin: clients papers 14pp *Private*
31333 Smythe family of Barbavilla: family and estate papers 2pp *National L of Ireland*
31334 Synge family of Glanmore: family and estate papers 9pp *National L of Ireland*
31335 General Sir Richard Chambre Hayes Taylor: corresp and papers 18pp *Private*
31336 Tipping family of Bellurgan: family and estate papers 3pp *Private*
31337 Walker family of Fonthill Abbey: corresp and papers 3pp *Private*
31338 Weldon family, baronets, of Kilmorony: family and estate papers 2pp *National L of Ireland*
31339 India, Pakistan and Burma Association 51pp *India Office L*
31340 Woods family of Milverton: family and estate papers 8pp *Private*

31341 Missionary Settlement for University Women, Bombay 26pp *India Office L*

31342 Archibald Ian Bowman, Indian civil servant: corresp and papers 10pp *India Office L*

31343 Captain Cyril Grey Snelling, Indian Political Service: diaries and papers 5pp *India Office L*

31344 Henry Peter Brougham, 1st Baron Brougham and Vaux, statesman and James Brougham MP: corresp 41pp *Univ Coll London*

31345 Lt-Colonel Donald Weir: corresp and papers 42pp *Leics RO*

31346 Warren family, baronets, of Warren House: deeds and papers 5pp *Private*

31347 St Columba's College, Rathfarnham 19pp *Private*

31348 Oliver family of Castle Oliver: family and estate papers 11pp *National L of Ireland*

31349 Lloyd family of Gloster: family and estate papers 9pp *National L of Ireland*

31350 Dublin: Kirwan and Pleasants Schools 5pp *National L of Ireland*

31351 Harty family, baronets, of Belrobin: family and estate papers 2pp *Private*

31352 Byrne family of Rosemount: family and estate papers 5pp *Private*

31353 Erck family of Sherrington: family and estate papers 3pp *National L of Ireland*

31354 De Burgh family of Oldtown: family and estate papers 12pp *Private*

31355 Darley family of Bray: family and estate papers 1p *Private*

31356 Colvill family of Coolock: family and estate papers 6pp *Private*

31357 Cobbe family of Newbridge: family and estate papers 1p *Private*

31358 Glascott family of Alderton: family and estate papers 3pp *National L of Ireland*

31359 Thompson family of Rathnally: family and estate papers 1p *Private*

31360 Molony family of Kiltanon: family and estate papers 4pp *National L of Ireland*

31361 Greene family of Gokane: corresp and papers 3pp *Private*

31362 Seymour family of Somerset House: family and estate papers 1p *Private*

31363 Brodigan family of Pilltown: family and estate papers 2pp *National L of Ireland*

31364 Sanders family of Charleville: family and estate papers 2pp *Private*

31365 Greene family of Millbrook: family and estate papers 3pp *Private*

31366 Pratt family of Cabra: family and estate papers 2pp *National L of Ireland*

31367 Aylmer family of Ayesha: family and estate papers 6pp *Private*

31368 Smyth family of Ballynegall: family and estate papers 2pp *National L of Ireland*

31369 Coalville & District Co-operative Society 2pp *Leics RO and Private*

31370 Trench family of Slane: corresp and papers 24pp *Private*

31371 Leicester: Glenfrith Hospital 9pp *Leics RO*

31372 British Fire Services Association: North Eastern district 2pp *Leics RO*

31373 Charles Moore & Sons, piano, gramophone and wireless dealers, South Wigston 4pp *Leics RO*

31374 William Cotton Ltd, hosiery machinery mfrs, Loughborough 4pp *Leics RO*

31375 Labour Party: Loughborough constituency 18pp *Leics RO*

31376 Birley & Co, cotton spinners and mfrs, Manchester 2pp *Univ of Florida L, Gainesville, USA*

31377 Blackburn and District Hospital Management Committee 3pp *Lancs RO*

31378 Bolton: St Mary of the Assumption Roman Catholic Church 3pp *Lancs RO*

31379 Nathan Ball & Son, clock and watch makers, Leicester 9pp *Leics RO*

31380 Lutterworth board of guardians 7pp *Leics RO*

31381 Wigston and Oadby Urban District Councils 10pp *Leics RO*

31382 JE Pickard & Sons Ltd, wool spinners, Leicester 50pp *Leics RO*

31383 Timms family of Odstone: business and family papers 25pp *Leics RO*

31384 Leicester General Hospital 1p *Leics RO*

31385 Leicester Quaker Housing Association Ltd 7pp *Leics RO*

31386 Leicester After-Care and Mental Deficiency Committees 5pp *Leics RO*

31387 Sanford family of Nynehead: family and estate papers 134pp *Somerset RO*

31388 Association of Jute Spinners and Manufacturers, Dundee 37pp *Dundee Univ L*

31389 Made-up Textiles Association, Dundee 3pp *Dundee Univ L*

31390 Sir Thomas Fife Clark, director-general, Central Office of Information: corresp and papers 20pp *Churchill Coll, Cambridge*

31391 John Burns Hynd MP: corresp and papers 19pp *Churchill Coll, Cambridge*

31392 Alfred Duff Cooper, 1st Viscount Norwich: corresp and papers 32pp *Churchill Coll, Cambridge*

31393 Admiral Sir Bertram Home Ramsay: corresp and papers 19pp *Churchill Coll, Cambridge*

31394 Sir Austin Robinson, economist: corresp and papers 37pp *Churchill Coll, Cambridge*

31395 Sir Dingle Foot MP, lawyer: corresp and papers 23pp *Churchill Coll, Cambridge*

31396 Maurice Pascal Alers Hankey, 1st Baron Hankey: corresp and papers 67pp *Churchill Coll, Cambridge*

31397 Archdeaconry of the East Riding 65pp *Borthwick Inst, York*

31398 Colonel Alexander Stalker Lancaster, military attaché in Kabul: corresp and papers 10pp *National Army Mus*

31399 Durham University: College of St Hild and St Bede 240pp *Durham RO*

31400 General Sir Andrew Thorne: corresp and papers 100pp *National Army Mus*

31401 Major-General Alexander Dury: corresp and papers 42pp *National Army Mus*

31402 Lt-General Sir Gerald Francis Ellison: corresp and papers 160pp *National Army Mus*

31403 Oakham Congregational Church 1p *Leics RO*

31404 Market Harborough United Reformed Church 2pp *Leics RO*

31405 Loughborough Baptist churches 1p *Leics RO*

31406 Leicester West Methodist Circuit 3pp *Leics RO*

31407 Alresford: Titchborne Down House Hospital 2pp *Hants RO*

31408 Basingstoke: Park Prewett Psychiatric Hospital 4pp *Hants RO*

31409 Rose & Alexander, ironmongers, Fordingbridge 3pp *Hants RO*

31410 Mouland family of Nether Wallop: family and estate papers 6pp *Hants RO*

31411 J Payne & Son, funeral directors, builders and decorators, Emery Down 13pp *Hants RO*

31412 Alton Rural Deanery 1p *Hants RO*

31413 Waddington family of Llanover Court: corresp 210pp *National L of Wales*

31414 Clement Davies, politician: corresp and papers 1001pp *National L of Wales*

31415 Buckley family of Castell Gorford: family and estate papers 21pp *National L of Wales*

31416 Davies and Charles families: corresp and papers 34pp *National L of Wales*

31417 Cardiganshire Quarter Sessions 11pp *National L of Wales*

31418 DR Davies: drama collection 43pp *National L of Wales*

31419 Cambrian Archaeological Association 29pp *National L of Wales*

31420 Crawshay family of Cyfarthfa: family, business and estate papers 1000pp *National L of Wales*

31421 J Wippell & Co Ltd, clerical outfitters, robe makers and church furnishers, Exeter 10pp *Private*

31422 Barnstaple: North Devon Friendly Institution 2pp *Devon RO, Barnstaple*

31423 Barnstaple: North Devon Athenaeum meteorological records 3pp *Devon RO, Barnstaple*

31424 Devon Record Office, Barnstaple: misc accessions 14pp *Devon RO, Barnstaple*

31425 Amesbury School, Hindhead 1p *Surrey RO, Guildford*

31426   Norwich Methodist Circuit 1p *Norfolk RO*

31427   Ingham and Stalham Baptist churches 4pp *Norfolk RO*

31428   Guildford: Archbishop Abbot's Hospital Manufactory 6pp *Surrey RO, Guildford*

31429   Liverpool Society of Anaesthetists 2pp *Liverpool Univ Archives*

31430   Drummond Bros Ltd, machine tool mfrs, Guildford 23pp *Surrey RO, Guildford*

31431   Bolton: St Patrick Roman Catholic Church 3pp *Lancs RO*

31432   Liverpool University Sociology Department social surveys 36pp *Liverpool Univ Archives*

31433   John Gunning & Son Ltd, linen mfrs, Cookstown 30pp *PRO of N Ireland*

31434   Greer family of Dungannon: family and business corresp and papers 216pp *PRO of N Ireland*

31435   Hale, Martin & Co Ltd, linen mfrs, Balnamore 8pp *PRO of N Ireland and Private*

31436   Richardson family of Bessbrook: family and estate papers 84pp *PRO of N Ireland*

31437   Banford Bleachworks Co Ltd, Gilford 35pp *PRO of N Ireland*

31438   Kilwee Bleaching Co, Dunmurry 6pp *PRO of N Ireland*

31439   J & W Charley & Co Ltd, linen mfrs, Dunmurry 29pp *PRO of N Ireland*

31440   Durham Street Weaving Co Ltd, linen mfrs, Belfast 30pp *PRO of N Ireland*

31441   William Kirk & Sons, linen mfrs, Keady 2pp *PRO of N Ireland*

31442   Belfast Flax & Jute Co Ltd 12pp *PRO of N Ireland*

31443   Edward Gribbon & Sons Ltd, linen mfrs, Coleraine 11pp *PRO of N Ireland*

31444   Broadway Damask Co, linen mfrs, Belfast 25pp *PRO of N Ireland*

31445   Gailey & Taylor, flax commission agents, Londonderry 2pp *PRO of N Ireland*

31446   William Coulson & Sons, linen mfrs, Lisburn 15pp *PRO of N Ireland*

31447   Island Spinning Co, linen mfrs, Lisburn 3pp *PRO of N Ireland*

31448   David Acheson Ltd, linen mfrs and finishers, Castlecaulfield 38pp *PRO of N Ireland*

31449   Hazelbank Weaving Co Ltd, linen mfrs, Laurencetown 4pp *PRO of N Ireland*

31450   Old Bleach Linen Co Ltd, linen mfrs, bleachers and merchants, Randalstown 6pp *PRO of N Ireland*

31451   Blackstaff Flax Spinning & Weaving Co Ltd, Belfast 7pp *PRO of N Ireland*

31452   Joseph Orr & Sons Ltd, linen mfrs, Benburb 8pp *PRO of N Ireland*

31453   Belleek Needlework and Sprigging Industry 12pp *PRO of N Ireland*

31454   Samuel McCrudden & Co (Belfast) Ltd, linen and handkerchief mfrs 8pp *PRO of N Ireland*

31455   HM Robb & Co Ltd, linen and handkerchief mfrs, Belfast 12pp *PRO of N Ireland*

31456   Sir Edward Mellanby, physiologist: corresp and papers 65pp *CMAC, Wellcome Inst*

31457   Glendinning, McLeish & Co, linen merchants, Belfast 56pp *PRO of N Ireland*

31458   James Campbell, flaxseed and linen agent, Belfast 6pp *PRO of N Ireland*

31459   SS Stott Ltd, conveyor mfrs, Haslingden 12pp *Lancs RO*

31460   Lancaster: St Thomas More Roman Catholic Church 1p *Lancs RO*

31461   Strain family of Ouley, co Down and Belfast: family and business papers 51pp *PRO of N Ireland*

31462   William Clarke & Sons, linen mfrs, Upperlands 7pp *PRO of N Ireland*

31463   Larne Weaving Co, linen mfrs 15pp *PRO of N Ireland*

31464   Belfast Ropeworks Co Ltd 9pp *PRO of N Ireland*

31465   George Walker & Co Ltd, flax and hemp spinners, Newtownards 3pp *PRO of N Ireland*

31466   Allen & Turtle Ltd, hosiery mfrs, dyers and finishers, Belfast 2pp *PRO of N Ireland*

31467   New Northern Spinning and Weaving Co Ltd, Belfast 8pp *PRO of N Ireland*

31468 Young & Anderson Ltd, wholesale woollen merchants and warehousemen, Belfast 14pp *PRO of N Ireland*

31469 Robinson & Cleaver Ltd, linen mfrs, merchants and general outfitters, London and Belfast 23pp *PRO of N Ireland*

31470 JN Richardson Sons & Owden, linen mfrs, Belfast 2pp *PRO of N Ireland*

31471 Miller, Boyd & Reid Ltd, wholesale textile and clothing distributors, Belfast 2pp *PRO of N Ireland*

31472 Lambeg Bleaching, Dyeing & Finishing Co 19pp *PRO of N Ireland*

31473 Anthony Cowdy & Sons Ltd, linen mfrs and bleachers, Banbridge 3pp *PRO of N Ireland*

31474 Pendle District School Games Association 1p *Lancs RO*

31475 William Liddell & Co Ltd, linen and damask mfrs, Donaghcloney 5pp *PRO of N Ireland*

31476 Raceview Woollen Mills, Broughshane 23pp *PRO of N Ireland*

31477 Henderson & Eadie, woollen mfrs, Lisbellaw 14pp *PRO of N Ireland*

31478 Ulster Woollen Co Ltd, Crumlin 76pp *PRO of N Ireland*

31479 Phoenix Weaving Co, linen mfrs, Ballymena 15pp *PRO of N Ireland*

31480 Raphael family of Galgorm: family, estate and business papers 8pp *PRO of N Ireland*

31481 Kirkpatrick Bros, bleachers, dyers and finishers, Ballyclare 29pp *PRO of N Ireland*

31482 Hillsborough Linen Co Ltd 10pp *PRO of N Ireland*

31483 National Society of Metal Mechanics 30pp *Warwick University Modern Records Centre*

31484 Union of Insurance Staffs 27pp *Warwick University Modern Records Centre*

31485 Transport Development Group plc: records of constituent companies 20pp *Warwick University Modern Records Centre*

31486 Engineering Employers East Midlands Association 29pp *Warwick University Modern Records Centre*

31487 Gillott Motors Ltd, motor dealers, Sheffield 2pp *Warwick University Modern Records Centre*

31488 Berkshire Clergy Charity Trust 6pp *Berks RO*

31489 Berkshire Nurses and Relief in Sickness Trust 6pp *Berks RO*

31490 John Thornton, evangelical: journals 2pp *Greater London RO*

31491 Ealing Borough 41pp *Greater London RO*

31492 London: Whitechapel Mission 135pp *Greater London RO*

31493 Wadworth & Co Ltd, brewers, Devizes 8pp *Private*

31494 Aquascutum Group PLC, clothing mfrs and retailers, London 13pp *Private*

31495 Plymouth: Moorhaven Hospital 6pp *Devon RO, Plymouth*

31496 RB Tope & Co Ltd, tent mfrs and contractors, Plymouth 2pp *Devon RO, Plymouth*

31497 Bond family of Castlelyons: family and estate papers 2pp *Private*

31498 Fetherstonhaugh & Carter, solicitors, Mountrath 2pp *Private*

31499 Fowler family of Rahinston: family and estate papers 3pp *National L of Ireland and Private*

31500 Dublin and Kildare diocese 6pp *Trinity Coll L, Dublin and Private*

31501 Pollock family of Mountainstown: family and estate papers 2pp *Private*

31502 Harefield Methodist Church 3pp *Greater London RO*

31503 H Temple Phillips, physician: corresp and papers 19pp *Bristol RO*

31504 Furnell family of Ballyclough: family and estate papers 3pp *Private*

31505 Clonmel Borough 2pp *Private*

31506 Keatinge family of Woodsgift: corresp and papers 9pp *Private*

31507 Blood family of Adelphi: family and estate papers 1p *Private*

31508 Hutchins family of Ballylicky and Ardnagashel: family and estate papers 4pp *Private*

31509 Dublin: King's Hospital 2pp *National L of Ireland*

31510 Godfrey family, baronets, of Ballinagroun: family and estate papers 29pp *Private*

31511 Prittie family, Barons Dunalley: family and estate papers 5pp *National L of Ireland*

31512 Hayes family of Crosshaven: family and estate papers 2pp *Private*

31513 Hodder family of Fountainstown: family and estate papers 1p *Private*

31514 Stoney family of Currabinny: family and estate papers 2pp *Private*

31515 Butler family of Priestown: family and estate papers 22pp *Private*

31516 Gollock family of Forest: family and estate papers 5pp *Private*

31517 Kildare Dean and Chapter 2pp *Private*

31518 Allen family of Clashenure: family and estate papers 2pp *Private*

31519 Holroyd-Smith family of Ballynatray: family and estate papers 2pp *National L of Ireland*

31520 Stratford family, Earls of Aldborough: family and estate papers 3pp *National L of Ireland*

31521 Franks & Oulton, solicitors, Dublin: clients' papers 1p *Univ Coll, Dublin*

31522 William Conyngham Plunket, 1st Baron Plunket, Lord Chancellor of Ireland: corresp 2pp *National L of Ireland*

31523 Synnott family of Furness: family and estate papers 7pp *Private*

31524 Ledwich family of Kilrathmurry: corresp and papers 2pp *National L of Ireland*

31525 Cassidy family of Monastereven: corresp 1p *National L of Ireland*

31526 French family, Barons De Freyne: family and estate papers 2pp *National L of Ireland*

31527 Crouch End: Ferme Park Baptist Church 4pp *Greater London RO*

31528 Bury family of Downings: family and estate papers 4pp *Private*

31529 Maynooth: St Patrick's College 62pp *Private*

31530 Butler family, baronets, of Cloughgrenan: family and estate papers 2pp *Private*

31531 Limerick City Museum: MS collection 3pp *Private*

31532 O'Brien family, Barons Inchiquin: corresp and papers 1p *National L of Ireland*

31533 London: Parmiter's Foundation 48pp *Greater London RO*

31534 Lloyds Bank Ltd: Guernsey branch 1p *Lloyds Bank Archives*

31535 Courage Ltd, brewers 26pp *Private*

31536 Wolverhampton: Civic Hall Arts Society 6pp *Wolverhampton Central L*

31537 National Society of Metal Mechanics: Wolverhampton branch 1p *Wolverhampton Central L*

31538 Alfred Hinde Ltd, printers, Wolverhampton 2pp *Wolverhampton Central L*

31539 Edwin Hill & Son, estate agents Bilston 3pp *Wolverhampton Central L*

★31540 Sir Alister Clavering Hardy, zoologist: corresp and papers 100pp *Bodleian L, Oxford*

31541 Graham Pollard, bibliographer: corresp and papers incl records of Birrell & Garnett Ltd, booksellers 70pp *Bodleian L, Oxford*

31542 Harvey & Son (Lewes) Ltd, brewers 15pp *Private*

31543 TD Ridley & Sons Ltd, brewers, Chelmsford 2pp *Private*

31544 St Austell Brewery Co Ltd 12pp *Private*

31545 SA Brain & Co Ltd, brewers, Cardiff 10pp *Private*

31546 Hardys & Hanson plc, brewers, Nottingham 26pp *Private*

31547 Lloyd Griffith family of Tremadoc: family and business papers 58pp *Gwynedd Archives Service, Caernarfon*

31548 Isaac Gaunt Ltd, worsted spinners, Stanningley 1p *Leeds District Archives*

31549 Benjamin Webster, actor and dramatist: corresp 3pp *Westminster Archives Dept*

31550 Gypsy Lore Society 7pp *Liverpool Univ L*

31551 Dora Esther Yates, Romany scholar: corresp and papers 2pp *Liverpool Univ L*

31552 Robert Boyle, natural philosopher and chemist: papers 39pp *Royal Soc*

31553 National Society's Training College of Domestic Subjects, Hampstead 42pp *Greater London RO*

31554 Mitchells of Lancaster (Brewers) Ltd 9pp *Private*

31555 Clarke, Cluley & Co Ltd, aeronautical engineers and agricultural machinery mfrs, Kenilworth 8pp *Coventry City RO*

*31556 Robert William Ditchburn, physicist: corresp and papers 63pp *Reading Univ L and Liverpool Univ Archives*

31557 Andrew Park Hume, Indian civil servant: corresp and papers 22pp *India Office L*

31558 Caernarfon: Moriah Calvinistic Methodist Chapel 373pp *Gwynedd Archives Service, Caernarfon*

31559 Llandudno Urban District Council 19pp *Gwynedd Archives Service, Caernarfon*

31560 Llandudno Public Library: local history collection 100pp *Gwynedd Archives Service, Caernarfon*

31561 David Lloyd Rees, nonconformist minister, Talysarn: papers 90pp *Gwynedd Archives Service, Caernarfon*

31562 William Douglas, bookseller, Edinburgh: MS collection 134pp *Scottish RO*

31563 Vans Agnew family of Barnbarroch: family and estate papers 20pp *Scottish RO*

31564 William Moir Bryce: MS collection 42pp *Scottish RO*

31565 Fleming family, Earls of Wigtown: family and estate papers 141pp *National L of Scotland*

31566 Duff family of Fetteresso: family and estate papers 87pp *Scottish RO*

31567 James Brown Craven, archdeacon: Orkney collection 65pp *Scottish RO*

31568 Tulloch family of Tannachie: family and estate papers 35pp *Scottish RO*

31569 Leslie family of Pitcaple: deeds and papers 22pp *Scottish RO*

31570 Society of Antiquaries of Scotland: MS collection 196pp *Scottish RO and Royal Mus of Scotland, Antiquities*

31571 Scott family of Raeburn: family and estate papers 32pp *Scottish RO*

31572 Tyne and Wear County Council Members Secretariat 2pp *Tyne and Wear Archives Dept*

31573 London County Council 60pp *Greater London RO*

31574 Stuart Rendel, Baron Rendel: business corresp and papers 12pp *Tyne and Wear Archives Dept and National L of Wales*

31575 John Hall & Sons (Bristol & London) Ltd, paint mfrs 9pp *Bristol RO*

31576 Bristol: Lewin's Mead Meeting (Unitarian) 22pp *Bristol RO*

31577 Bristol Adult School Union 2pp *Bristol RO*

31578 Congregational Union of Gloucestershire and Herefordshire: Bristol district 1p *Bristol RO*

31579 Eastwood Congregational Church 13pp *Calderdale District Archives*

31580 Herbert Gladstone Hendy, solicitor, Bristol 2pp *Bristol RO*

31581 Halifax charities 8pp *Calderdale District Archives*

31582 Reuben Gaunt & Sons Ltd, yarn spinners and worsted mfrs, Farsley 5pp *Leeds District Archives*

31583 David Dixon & Son Ltd, woollen mfrs, Leeds 4pp *Leeds District Archives*

31584 Arthur Harrison & Co Ltd, worsted mfrs, Leeds 5pp *Leeds District Archives*

31585 G & R Robinson & Co Ltd, linen, sack and carpet mfrs, Leeds 7pp *Leeds District Archives*

31586 Rawdon Low Mill Co 2pp *Leeds District Archives*

31587 General Sir Frederick Augustus Wetherall and General Sir George Augustus Wetherall: corresp and papers 15pp *National Army Mus*

31588 Bristol Permanent Economic Building Society 15pp *Bristol RO*

31589 Bristol: Knowle Park United Reformed Church 9pp *Bristol RO*

31590 George Swindells & Son Ltd, cotton mfrs, Bollington: family and business papers 15pp *Cheshire RO*

31591 Foot family of Pencrebar: misc corresp and papers 6pp *Devon RO, Plymouth*

31592 Plympton St Mary board of guardians 3pp *Devon RO, Plymouth*

31593 Plymouth, Devonport & Stonehouse Cemetery Co 2pp *Devon RO, Plymouth*

31594 Isaac Foot MP: misc corresp and papers 6pp *Devon RO, Plymouth*

31595 National Library of Wales: MSS rel to Brittany 16pp *National L of Wales*

★31596 Gwen John, painter: corresp and papers 85pp *National L of Wales*

31597 Ermington Charities Feoffees 16pp *Devon RO, Plymouth*

31598 Essex Record Office, Colchester: misc accessions 250pp *Essex RO, Colchester*

31599 Hamilton-Dalrymple family, baronets, of North Berwick: family and estate papers 177pp *Scottish RO*

31600 Alexander Ormiston Curle, archaeologist: MS collection 26pp *Scottish RO*

31601 Campbell family, Earls of Breadalbane: family and estate papers 324pp *Scottish RO*

31602 Innes family of Stow: family and estate papers 13pp *Scottish RO*

31603 Campbell family of Duntroon, Argyllshire: deeds and papers 73pp *Scottish RO*

31604 Cathcart family, baronets, of Carleton: family and estate papers 36pp *Scottish RO*

31605 Cheltenham District Health Authority 1p *Glos RO*

31606 Risbridge board of guardians 15pp *Suffolk RO, Bury St Edmunds*

31607 Bury St Edmunds: Fennell Memorial Homes 8pp *Suffolk RO, Bury St Edmunds*

31608 Bardwell charities 5pp *Suffolk RO, Bury St Edmunds*

31609 Brandon and District Aid-in-Sickness Fund 4pp *Suffolk RO, Bury St Edmunds*

31610 Lakenheath: Goward and Evans charities 4pp *Suffolk RO, Bury St Edmunds*

31611 Stoke and Melford Union Association 2pp *Suffolk RO, Bury St Edmunds*

31612 Garrard family, builders, Lavenham: business and family papers 7pp *Suffolk RO, Bury St Edmunds*

31613 Stedman, solicitors, Sudbury and Pakenham 19pp *Suffolk RO, Bury St Edmunds*

31614 Quant & Son Ltd, boot and shoe makers and dealers, Bury St Edmunds 7pp *Suffolk RO, Bury St Edmunds*

31615 Bullen family of Bury St Edmunds: corresp and papers 8pp *Suffolk RO, Bury St Edmunds*

31616 Burnett & Reid, solicitors, Aberdeen: clients papers 15pp *Private*

31617 Archibald Young & Son Ltd, surgical instrument makers, Edinburgh 5pp *Private*

31618 Gray family of Roeberry: family and estate papers 22pp *Orkney AO*

31619 Kirkwall: St Olaf's Episcopal Church 16pp *Orkney AO*

31620 Hugh Marwick, historian and educationalist: corresp and papers 29pp *Orkney AO*

31621 William Hugh Clifford Frend, ecclesiastical historian : corresp and papers 15pp *Glasgow Univ Archives*

31622 William Christopher Atkinson, professor of Hispanic studies, Glasgow: literary papers 5pp *Glasgow Univ Archives*

31623 Murray Johnstone Holdings (1984) Ltd, Glasgow 7pp *Private*

31624 Cox Brothers, jute mfrs, Dundee 22pp *Dundee Archive Centre*

31625 Philip Ivor Dee, physicist: diaries and papers 6pp *Glasgow Univ Archives*

31626 DV Marshall, surgeon: corresp and papers 5pp *Glasgow Univ Archives*

31627 Thomas Aitken, physicist: papers 4pp *Glasgow Univ Archives*

31628 Jesmond United Reformed Church 28pp *Tyne and Wear Archives Dept*

31629 South Shields: St Margaret United Reformed Church 7pp *Tyne and Wear Archives Dept*

31630 Wilson family of Forest Hall: family and estate papers 51pp *Tyne and Wear Archives Dept*

31631 Ryton United Reformed Church 9pp *Tyne and Wear Archives Dept*

31632 Wideopen: St John United Reformed Church 15pp *Tyne and Wear Archives Dept*

31633 Austin & Pickersgill Ltd, shipbuilders, Sunderland 4pp *Durham RO*

31634 Villiers-Stuart family of Dromana: deeds 34pp *Herts RO*

31635 George Bateman & Son Ltd, brewers, Wainfleet 12pp *Private*

31636 Swalwell United Reformed Church 21pp *Tyne and Wear Archives Dept*

31637 Manchester Poetical Society 3pp *Manchester Central L*

31638 Manchester and Salford Shaftesbury Society 8pp *Manchester Central L*

31639 North Western Ironfounders Employers Association 2pp *Manchester Central L*

31640 Manchester: Northenden Civic Society 6pp *Manchester Central L*

31641 Manchester Grammar School 7pp *Manchester Central L*

31642 Manchester: Baguley Sanatorium 2pp *Manchester Central L*

31643 United Manchester Hospitals 3pp *Manchester Central L*

31644 Plymouth District Baptist churches 2pp *Devon RO, Plymouth*

31645 Devonport: Hope Baptist Church 1p *Devon RO, Plymouth*

31646 Ford Baptist Church 3pp *Devon RO, Plymouth*

31647 Plympton charities 1p *Devon RO, Plymouth*

31648 Hull Literary and Philosophical Society 4pp *Hull City RO*

31649 Hull Mechanics Institute 4pp *Hull City RO*

31650 Waunfawr Calvinistic Methodist Chapel 18pp *Gwynedd Archives Service, Caernarfon*

*31651 John Leonard Jinks, geneticist: corresp and papers 15pp *Birmingham Univ L*

31652 Abbotsbury United Reformed Church 5pp *Dorset RO*

31653 Cerne Abbas United Reformed Church 9pp *Dorset RO*

31654 Extract Wool Manufacturing Ltd, shoddy and mungo mfrs, Dewsbury 14pp *Leeds District Archives*

31655 George Dutton (Northwich) Ltd, roller leather dressers 7pp *Cheshire RO*

31656 Brocklehurst Whiston Amalgamated Ltd, silk mfrs, Langley 8pp *Cheshire RO*

31657 Taverham petty sessions 2pp *Norfolk RO*

31658 Blofield and Walsham petty sessions 1p *Norfolk RO*

31659 Loddon Methodist Circuit 3pp *Norfolk RO*

31660 East Anglia Methodist District 1p *Norfolk RO*

31661 Norfolk Freemasons: Francis of Lorraine Lodge (no 6906) 1p *Norfolk RO*

31662 South Shields: St Paul and St John United Reformed Church 28pp *Tyne and Wear Archives Dept*

31663 National and Local Government Officers Association: Gateshead branch 3pp *Tyne and Wear Archives Dept*

31664 St Andrew's Permanent Building Society, Newcastle upon Tyne 11pp *Tyne and Wear Archives Dept*

31665 Northumberland Park Bowling Club 3pp *Tyne and Wear Archives Dept*

31666 Sunderland: George Hudson's Charity 19pp *Tyne and Wear Archives Dept*

31667 Gomshall United Reformed Church 3pp *Surrey RO, Guildford*

31668 Scott-Ellis family, Barons Howard de Walden: St Marylebone estate papers 4pp *Westminster Archives Dept, Marylebone*

Principal replacements of and additions to existing reports included:

10 Paget family, Marquesses of Anglesey: family and estate papers 104 pp *Staffs RO*

850 Gordon Lennox family, Dukes of Richmond and Gordon: family and estate papers[1] 169pp *W Sussex RO*

1083 Wentworth-Fitzwilliam family, Earls Fitzwilliam: family and estate papers 146pp *Sheffield Central L*

7132 Wilberforce family: papers 21pp *Bodleian L, Oxford*

7153 Monson family, Barons Monson of Burton: family and estate papers 180pp *Lincs AO*

---

[1] *The Goodwood Estate Archives. A Catalogue*, 3, ed TJ McCann, 1984